BIBLICAL AUTHORITY
FOR MODERN PREACHING

Books by
CHARLES W. F. SMITH
Published by The Westminster Press

BIBLICAL AUTHORITY FOR MODERN PREACHING
THE JESUS OF THE PARABLES

Biblical Authority
for
Modern Preaching

by
CHARLES W. F. SMITH

Philadelphia
THE WESTMINSTER PRESS

LIBRARY OF CONGRESS CATALOG CARD No. 60–7190

CONTENTS

Preface   7

  I. Is Preaching Outmoded?   11

 II. Or Is Preaching Essential?   32

III. The Ordering of Biblical Preaching   55

IV. Preacher, Bible, and People   80

 V. The Claim of the Bible on the Preacher   101

VI. The Claim of the People on the Preacher   122

Epilogue: Getting Started   147

Book List and References   170

PREFACE

"New occasions teach new duties." They also call for a review of old duties. There is little need for another book on preaching. A new look, however, at the task as it relates to its place in worship and at both as they are brought under discipline to the Bible seems to be called for in relation to the times. The remarkable growth in all the churches of interest in "liturgical revival," or "renewal," has within it an enlarging interest in Biblical preaching and in the relation of the ministry of the Word to the ministry of the sacraments. This interest is not confined to Protestant churches nor to any one country. Since these chapters were written, there has become available the testimony of Prof. J.-D. Benoit in his survey, *Liturgical Renewal*. The movement has justified the publication of a series of Studies in Ministry and Worship (of which Dr. Benoit's book is one) and of the series Ecumenical Studies in Worship.

Coincident with liturgical renewal and a revived interest in Biblical preaching, there have matured developments in the techniques of mass communication, in the involvement of the individual in group discussion, and the technical debate about "demythologizing." All of these

7

call attention to the minister's task. Their tendency is to make it seem an anomaly and him an anachronism. Professor Benoit's comment applies far beyond the context in which he made it: " Sometimes ministers take advantage of the fact that they cannot be answered back, and are severer than they ought to be, or else let themselves go with a gusto that is quite out of place " (p. 102).

The writer has no special competence to discuss these matters. (Such discussions may be found in the list of books added.) Hence, these chapters deal not so much with methods as with origins, not so much with " gimmicks " as with resources, not with a new content but with a new situation. To understand better what we are up against should send us back with renewed understanding to the basic resources of the Christian faith, there to discover anew the relevance of the authority of the Bible to a world in which the needs are the same, no matter how differently expressed, but in which the way they are expressed can effectively conceal any authority or relevance that might be found.

The attempts to apply this will be found by each reader the least satisfactory thing written, and to some the examples will seem ill-chosen. This is as it should be. They are not intended to be sermon suggestions, since every man who is called to the work is, by that call, obligated under God to solve the problem for himself and for his people in his own way — one might even better say, in their way.

An invitation to address the clergy of the Episcopal Diocese of Missouri in September, 1958, gave me occasion to put into the form of lectures material that had developed in this direction in the course of teaching and discussion over some fifteen years. These were somewhat extended before the class of 1959 at The Episcopal Theological School in Cambridge, Massachusetts, as a parallel to their practice-preaching. I am grateful to the Bishop of Missouri (Dr. Lichtenberger, now Presiding Bishop) for the opportunity, to the clergy of Missouri for their penetrating discussions, and to the class of 1959 for their sympathetic hearing. An attempt has been made to avoid discussions that would relate to the practice of any one church or to only liturgical churches.

It has been my good fortune to alternate the practice of preaching regularly with opportunities to hear and discuss sermons, an opportunity not often available to the active minister. I have benefited from listening to student sermons in two seminaries, to sermons by ministers from the field at the College of Preachers, by a succession of leading exponents in my days as a curate in Richmond, Virginia, and as a canon at the Washington Cathedral, by English clergy and some French on two sabbatical leaves, and by discussions when in residence at St. Augustine's College, Canterbury, England, with ministers from places that are as remote as Nigeria, Egypt, India, and New Guinea.

If the pages that follow seem sometimes critical, it is not from lack of appreciation of the difficulties of the task (under which I myself have labored). Rather, it appears to me necessary to define more closely what is the real task and the most reliable support of the preacher of the gospel and exponent of the Christian way of life. It is my conviction that many of the deficiencies of preaching come from attempting too much, and attempting it without the support and illumination that is available in an ordered use of the Word of God. If the analysis here attempted can at least remove complacency, ease discouragement, and disturb routine, its purpose will have been accomplished. A willingness to begin anew is always honored by him who said, "My word shall not return to me empty."

CHARLES W. F. SMITH

Cambridge, Massachusetts

I

IS PREACHING OUTMODED?

Is THERE any place for the sermon in the second half of the twentieth century? This question is part of the larger inquiry concerning the relevance of Christianity and the churches. A discussion of the sermon enables us to deal with some aspects of this question where it affects the contact of the Christian community with the world. The pressure of the world on the churches has created problems for the preacher that are new in their form and impact. Little fresh can profitably be said about preaching as an art, but the examination of the question, Why preach at all today? will reveal that an age-old discipline needs re-examination.

There are four particular points at which the world forces upon the churches the reconsideration of this question. *First,* the methods of so-called group dynamics developed in industry have had their effect upon the function and method of Christian education and communication of the gospel in general within the churches. This raises the question in the form, Is the sermon an outmoded *method?* Here we are compelled to ask whether preaching as such has some particular justification within the Christian enterprise and, if so, what sort of thing is preaching so understood.

The *second* is another impact of the world's advance,

namely, the effects of the scientific method of investigation of all phenomena, here in particular applied to the
traditions and symbols of the Christian faith. At this point
Dr. Bultmann has taken the lead in stating the issue with
his proposals for demythologizing the gospel. Can a religion that developed its traditions in an age of mythological thinking still make its voice heard in an age when
all modes of thought are dominated by scientific realism?
Here the form of the question about preaching is whether
it can adapt itself as a means of bringing home to modern
man the essential encounter between God and man in
Christ, which in the beginning expressed itself in a form
no longer available to us.

The *third* point of impact is a more general form of the
second, and may be called the whole " ethos " of modern
life. Here the question must, for us, be asked particularly
in the form of the American ethos. The unexamined and
often unrealized basic assumptions of the modern American seem, as they meet us every day, remote in the extreme from any basis of motivation congenial to the Christian gospel and way of life. This is becoming increasingly
true far beyond America as Western industrialism spreads
to Africa and the East. An entirely new situation obtains
for which there is little precedent to be found in history
or any previous culture. The means of communication
that have been developed, the uses to which they are put,
the effect they are having in scope and depth, and the
ends for which they might be used constitute not only a
problem for the success of preaching but also an actual
threat to the whole undertaking of which preaching is the
expressive part. The impact here has made itself felt upon
the preacher. He often, without realizing it, has suc-
cumbed to the very same ethos and finds difficulty in

making essential distinctions between church and world, between salvation and success, between gospel and propaganda.

A *fourth* point might be called the loss of the preacher's audience. The preacher's predicament in this regard is a result of the impact of the factors already mentioned and of the unreality of the existence of the churches in the world that confronts us. This unreality is not always felt at the local level, where a sort of "church boom" is in progress, an ecclesiastical prosperity that for the time being veils the situation. The time is already more than ripe to look beyond this apparently favorable situation and prepare to analyze it a little more realistically.

The preaching of sermons as generally conceived involves a minister ordained by his church to preach, standing before a congregation and delivering to it a spoken discourse as part of a service of worship. In this process the preacher speaks without interruption or immediate comment from his audience upon a theme about which it has not been consulted. No check is made, as a rule, upon his selection of a subject or upon the effectiveness with which he performs what appears to be expected of him beyond the freedom of people (in the Protestant churches) to absent themselves. This they do in large numbers. Those who attend are usually in some sense "members" of the church involved and provide the means whereby the preacher is free to devote his time to the functions of his ministry, however these functions may be conceived. The implication is that a kind of authority is inherent in the function of the minister in the pulpit that he takes for granted as justifying his right to speak unchallenged. This inherent authority his hearers appear to accept without protest.

It is really an odd undertaking in the modern world. The question is, Does it fit, and can it, or should it, survive? The kind of communication involved appears from modern studies to be wasteful because ineffective. The experiments conducted among groups indicate that some measurement of the effectiveness of what is done is necessary if it is to continue to be done with effect. Studies of learning and of the kind of apprehension that leads to changed viewpoints and redirected activities have shown that there must be expression on the part of the recipients — whether by discussion among themselves or with the speaker or by a response that is expected to arise from previous " conditioning." This conditioning itself can be shown to be effective only by being given expression.

The average churchgoer has, whether he realizes it or not, certain sanctions in his hands. He can avoid being spoken to "from above" by staying away. He can continue to come but can exert pressure through whatever governing body is available to have the particular minister removed. This depends upon the church — in some it is easily done, and in others it cannot be done at all except for grave cause. This last sanction, however, does not solve the problem of being preached to without recourse. One preacher is removed only for another to take his place. No layman can be entirely sure that a minister chosen with his approval will not sooner or later say something with which he disagrees or will find objectionable if taken seriously.

Here is a qualification that reveals the real question of preaching. The verb " preach " itself has come to have the connotation of something unreal and improperly demanding, which, therefore, need *not* be taken seriously. The most urgent problems about preaching arise from its ac-

ceptance as a performance that is satisfied in the performing. The question about the sermon arises most seriously
from the fact that the question is not asked at all. Preaching has been taken for granted. One can go and hear a
sermon (as he can go and worship with others) or not as
he pleases, and in most places no penalty or obloquy results. It is strictly for those who like that sort of thing. In
other words, the authority that the process of preaching
implies by the way it is conducted is an authority that is
not widely accepted and is not even recognized by those
who submit themselves to it. The grounds offered for
hearing sermons by those who do hear them will seldom
(never in my own experience) justify the hearing by reference to the authority inherent in the ministerial function.

Would it not be wise, then, to discontinue the sermon
(or at least confine it to special occasions) and substitute
for it some form of group activity in which the minister's
function would be only to a small extent that of preacher?
The question is not intended to be a frivolous one. The
change would provide valuable material for study if a
number of ministers would, for a time or on periodic occasions, substitute for the sermon something in the nature
of a discussion. The results could then be studied against
the control of a serious attempt to find out what the congregation's response is to sermons heard in the ordinary
way. In such an experiment the minister might propose
the topic and introduce it, though he might do this as a
result of the decision of a " steering committee " of which
he would be or would not be a member. He might act as
moderator of the discussion or as a reconvener of the several groups into which the participants might be divided
for preliminary discussion ("buzz groups"). He might,

instead, act as a " resource person," exercising an authority dependent entirely on his more complete information or understanding — an authority that would carry its own authentication apart from the apparatus of a church that ordains.

The results would be interesting, even astonishing, in more ways than one. Here we need only observe that the function of the preacher in the usual sense would have disappeared. His normal function would be almost entirely gone because his descent from the pulpit into the forum and his surrender of the role of sole speaker would betoken his surrender of authority. (In many cases this would logically carry with it the need to divest himself of any robes of office.)

We therefore see that in some way the role of the minister as a preacher of sermons is in itself the manifestation of an authority that differentiates him from the hearers of sermons. Apart from that, the question of effectiveness in communicating the gospel remains unaffected. Indeed, probably a good case could be made for the superior effectiveness of many methods other than that of preaching in the communication of the gospel — assuming always that it is *that*, communication, and not, for example, entertainment that is being sought. This is particularly true if entertainment is not the real end but the encouragement and enabling of a way of life in those who hear sermons, a way increasingly to be distinguished from the way of life of those who do not hear sermons. The great means of mass communication — movies, radio, and television, not to say printed matter of a periodical or daily nature — depend for their success, measured by economic survival, upon entertaining in some form. This is true even if the entertainment provided is interest at one end or shock at the other, with diversion as the middle and constant term.

A serious aspect of the preacher's predicament is the failure of the Christian church to retain the advance position in Western civilization that it has sometimes enjoyed. It could be argued that just as education itself was maintained in the Dark Ages by the church, so the advance into the field of literary and historical criticism was stimulated by the investigation of the Biblical literature. To an extent larger than the ordinary layman supposes, the "criticism" of the Bible and of the thought-forms of Christian discourse have arisen within the church. One reason the layman is unaware of this is that it is not evident in the pulpit. We have too often heard men who, trained in modern methods and competent in the classroom, show no signs whatever of this achievement when they undertake to preach. It is not to be expected (far from it) that they should parade their learning or impose upon their listeners the exegetical methods of modern research. The pulpit is no place for this. When it is used for this purpose, its already pressing problems are aggravated. What is lacking is any sign of such results as might manifest themselves in an awareness of the distance between the Biblical voice and the modern ear. Lacking also is any success in the translation of the religious idiom into the contemporary, able to manifest itself by the disclosure of a point of relevant application. The double duty of analysis that this imposes will be taken up later, but here we merely note the task that the preacher competent to undertake it has neglected.

The idiom of the Biblical source material and its complication in theological development is not merely a matter of words. As Bultmann, Wedel, and others have suggested, the whole world view of Christian revelation is remote from a world of thought dominated (rightly or wrongly) by a scientific viewpoint. To those (like the logical positivists) who expect controlled and limited statements about the nature of reality such as derive from experimental observation or strictly logical deduction, the whole realm of discourse in which religion moves is either incomprehensible or ludicrous. A divine history that at its most crucial points resorts to the mythological if not to the mythical is not, *in that form,* going to make much impact upon modern man, largely because it makes no in-itial point of contact at all. There are two exceptions, both of which make matters worse. The first is that a point of contact will be made, but it will be with stories, associa-tions, and attitudes of childhood. Since one of the pur-poses of preaching would seem to be the nurturing of religious maturity, this tendency to retrogress and to rein-force the childlike is opposed to the preacher's purpose, even if it does not cause the hearer to dismiss the whole business as something long ago outgrown. The listener associates it not only with his own childhood but very possibly with the childhood of the race. The second ex-ception is the case in which the hearer has been trained to accept on authority anything said by the church and to suspend, in this connection, his critical judgment. The training involves a separation between this realm of dis-course and all the others he uses, between what religion expects of him by way of " religious " activity and what controls the rest of his life. It should be obvious that the imposition of remote forms of thought by authority de-feats the very aim of the Christian gospel, which is to make a man whole, not to divide his life into watertight compartments, to save him by making a man of him and not by divorcing his soul from his body or his life in the church from his life in the world.

A potent sign of the failure to grapple with the problem and solve it is the retreat of the preacher into moralism. The sermons of several decades past have dealt largely in this currency, finding a ready hearing in the willingness of people to be told to be respectable or to follow the good life as conceived by all moralists of whatever religion (or none). A striking picture and trenchant examination of the moralistic message so congenial to an urban and industrialized society that admires the " self-made man " has been given by T. O. Wedel in his book *The Christianity of Main Street*. He shows how in this undertaking the very distinctiveness of the gospel is lost. The widespread assumption that this is what the Christian faith is really about is both the result of a mistaken cure and a further barrier to the hearing of the gospel.

In recent years there has been reaction — sometimes the violent one of the recrudescence of an evangelical fundamentalism. Where this has been avoided, the effort has been made to " rediscover " theology and to reclaim it for the pulpit. A danger here has been the adoption of an existentialist approach that easily develops into an anthropology with little or no real contact with theology, much less the gospel. I put it this way because it is quite possible for theology to enter the pulpit without having any real effect upon preaching because it is not *preached* theology — and sometimes not a preachable theology. We shall consider later the obligation to be theological, but at this point it is necessary to observe that much as the pulpit needs to rediscover theology, so, equally urgently, does theology need to rediscover the pulpit. That is to say, if the real advances in theological thinking (which can be broadly brought under the heading " existential ") are to be effective beyond the ranks of trained theologians, these advances must take seriously the problem of communication. Dr. Wedel has observed: " The church's pulpit, therefore, must stand guard over the saving gospel. The church's learned doctors need us, as we need them. Our protest against the tyranny of the intellect can save them from turning the Christian faith into an esoteric academic cult," *The Pulpit Rediscovers Theology* (p. 80). The task facing the preacher in the pulpit imposes upon the theologian the obligation to examine and continually to restate his doctrine until it meets the demands of the apologetic task.

The discipline designated " apologetics" is really the bridge between the study and the pulpit, between seminary and parish. One sometimes wonders whether some of the best students in our theological schools do not retreat into further studies in despair at the apologetic task that they, more than the less gifted, realize is so pressing and so difficult. Unless we are to have a purely esoteric religion, the very best graduates must face and solve the task of bringing their understanding to the people. It need hardly be said that this is not a plea for the concentration of theological education upon techniques. It does imply, however, that the teaching of " homiletics " should be broadened to include the baffling problems of communication and confrontation in the modern world. It also suggests the need for a heightened awareness on the part of those who teach the basic disciplines of Bible, church history, and theology, that their material is to be the background and also the content of the pastoral function of the pulpit. In no basic subject can the apologetic aspect be ignored. The words of Phillips Brooks, in his *Lectures on Preaching*, are still valid: " The student preparing to be a preacher cannot learn truth as the mere student of theology for its own sake might do. He always feels it reaching out through him to the people to whom he is someday to carry it. . . . We can see that it must have its dangers. It will threaten the impartiality with which he will seek truth. It will tempt him to prefer those forms of truth which most easily lend themselves to didactic uses. . . . Against that danger the man meaning to be a preacher must be upon his guard, but he cannot avoid the danger by sacrificing the habit out of which the danger springs. He must receive truth as one who is to teach it " (Lecture II).

Here the term "apologetics" is used in a perhaps broader sense than that involved in an academic pursuit of the subject where it still survives as an item in the curriculum. Formal apologetics must, of course, deal with the differences between the Christian world view, its metaphysics, epistemology, psychology, and the like, and other and competing views of the nature of things. The Christian, or Biblical, philosophy of history must be distinguished from others. The old study called " Evidences " must be revived in a quite different form. But beyond all this lies the real apologetic task, the business of commending the gospel to modern man, even to the extent of persuading him to accept its disparity with all he knows and its criticism, implied or explicit, of the way of life that he accepts almost as if it were a law of nature. Once again a reference to Dr. Wedel's *The Christianity of Main Street* will suggest the nature of the apologetic necessary. It must start with a clear understanding of "what we are up against." The essence of the preacher's task as apologetic in nature brings us, inevitably, to the third point.

The term "post-Christian" has aptly been applied to

the mid-twentieth century. To live in a post-Christian culture is a very different matter from living in a pre-Christian culture. To some people Christianity — as they suppose it to be — has been found wanting. Others have never really known Christianity — except by a sort of " osmosis," an influence seeping into their lives from unidentified sources. These have not been brought up in Christian homes, have seldom attended church at an ordinary service, have not been taught in a Sunday school or in a church-centered day or boarding school. To them, and to many others who have not been so neglected, " religion " is a matter of personal idiosyncrasy. Some feel that it may be true for some people and not for others — that religious truth is a matter for the individual to decide, even to create. Their ideas of the Christian faith are impressions gained haphazardly and not checked by the kind of investigation the educated among them would give to a subject like atomic physics or to the relative merits of the current makes of automobiles. Sometimes they have taken a course in " comparative religions " without having attempted the practice of any of the religions studied. There are probably more religious illiterates than there are people who have knowingly rejected the faith. They are not all, by any means, outside the churches.

This, however, is only the beginning of the problem, a symptom. Western civilization as a whole has moved away from a Christian basis. Christendom, as such, no longer exists except as a vestigial remains in the form of state churches in Great Britain and Europe and can no longer be taken for granted as the core or determining factor of Western civilization. The churches have been slow to recognize this, but the sooner they do the more readily will their ordinances be adapted to the real situation. The tracing of this change or loss of orientation is a lengthy business and not to be attempted here. Ingredients are drawn from the Renaissance, the Reformation, deism, naturalism, romanticism, the growth of the national state, imperialism, isolationism, and, above all, the materialism developed by the Industrial Revolution. The history of this last practically coincides with the history of the United States as an independent nation and has brought, through "free enterprise," a scale of material prosperity and ability to exert power beyond its borders hitherto unknown.

The assumptions that the development of a fundamentally economic culture have imposed pervade the thinking and even the instincts of those who are involved in it. It requires a prodigious effort to imagine any other "way of life." There is no escape from this, unless by atomic destruction. The well-being of all nations presupposes the development of an industrial base or the means to participate in such a structure. Unless the preacher realizes this, he is not in a position to gauge the distance of modern man from the man of the Biblical or even the medieval period — the whole area of time in which the Christian faith was born and developed and in which its classic thought-forms were created. Modern assumptions, whether unexamined or analyzed, are not those of the Christian gospel and way of life.

Within this framework the hearer of sermons finds himself also conditioned by the impact of modern technological and business developments. As business has grown large and labor correspondingly, so government has necessarily reached more and more into the concerns of citizens — and the prospect is of still further encroachment. Modern warfare involves everyone increasingly at many points and not only during the actual hostilities. A man's freedom has always been conditioned by the tribe, society, or state, but never quite so clearly as in a modern democracy, where the real freedom achieved yet carries an individual responsibility unknown by slave or serf. It is to this man that the gospel must be addressed. The preacher must be aware of him as he is if he is to address him directly.

Still more, technology and business have recently produced a situation, particularly in America, that constitutes a threat to the ability to hear and appropriate the Christian message. A man or woman's business — and this applies more especially to the executive class to whom communities look largely for leadership — has come to determine very largely his or her way of life. The mushrooming of expense accounts enables people to indulge in a mode of living and entertainment that would not be possible on their immediate personal income, with a resulting relief to the family budget. Involved in this are "pressures" (if not "temptations") to indulge in drinking, in eating, in a heightened sexual atmosphere and freedom, leading almost inevitably to a distorted sense of values. The entertainment of clients or the being entertained as a client has introduced many new dimensions and, for one who wishes to control his way of living, produced many problems not so easily solved when the pressures are felt "in the line of duty." It is not a matter any more of simply keeping up with the Joneses but of keeping up with the company and with its competitors. Down the line also the growing involvement is felt — even the secretary or office boy is expected to share in the "Christmas party" (virtual profanation as it is of the season) and to contribute to occasions and causes through the office, rather than from home, out of a pay check already reduced by withholding taxes, social security, health insurance, union dues, and the like. The tendency to diminish home and church as bases and controlling factors is also indicated by the extent to which even the child is involved in group activities once centered in the home. When the office and school have finished with, let us say, Christmas or the community fund, what is there for the home to do that is not redundant and likely to produce the response, " What, again? " Furthermore, an element of regimentation has emerged to influence where and how a man lives, to insist on a pattern of behavior, and even to condition his attitudes by test. No preacher can speak to modern man effectively if he is unaware of the pressures indicated in the book *The Organization Man,* by William H. Whyte, Jr.

If this were the situation, it would be a problem difficult enough for Christian communication, but over and through it all is the effect of modern mass communication. Constantly and pervasively, if not directly, then, through the impact on family, friends, and neighbors, the individual is subjected to a saturation barrage of words and pictures, producing mental images that are insistent and well-nigh inescapable. An individual can evade it by direct contact if he so desires, but he cannot evade the general atmosphere. It is hardly possible in brief space to do more than list the means — radio, television, magazines, newspapers, book-selection clubs, paperbacks (with their covers), advertising, and surveys. The impact is a compound that makes preaching an entirely different problem.

While at first glance the conditions would appear to make sermons almost useless, they also, at a further look, make them all the more necessary and perhaps provide certain opportunities. The compound is one of slanted news, propaganda, hero-idolatry, success worship, sex pervasion, the domestication of violence, and a subtle and sinister dependence on others (whose numbers are terrifyingly few) for the creation of attitudes, tastes, and opinions. A tendency has become apparent to decide by the tabulation of statistical data the questions of right and wrong in which the assumption is involved that a descriptive count of those who engage in a given practice justifies the practice or at least makes it permissive and outside the strictures of a nonstatistical morality. When news and information were conveyed primarily by word of mouth, and manuscripts or printed sheets were available only to a few and in small quantity, each item was likely to receive consideration and prolonged discussion. Now the essence of communication is the instantaneous impression, the hit-and-run method, even the sneak attack on the unaware (see Vance Packard's *The Hidden Persuaders*). For the Christian what is explicitly said is serious enough. More threatening still is the pervasiveness of a set of values, unexpressed and undiscussed, that will not bear examination as a basis on which to build Christian life and community.

A particularly sinister feature in all this is the power and practice of "build-up." In the literary realm it is no longer possible to estimate the real worth of a book by its sales or its place on the best-seller list. Methods of promotion make all the difference and give to the task of the literary critic a difficulty akin to that which we are discussing for the preacher. "Personalities" also can be virtually created by the same methods, "built up" by promotion and publicity. The process is highly selective. Contacts of the public (visual and audial) with the person are "screened" to create the desired affect. The test of actual performance and person-to-person encounter are decidedly minimized. The method has been successful in its aim, and an actress need not be gifted at acting if she is properly (or improperly) publicized and her personality, as developed by the build-up, is projected on the movie or TV screen, carefully edited. It has also had an effect upon the democratic process, and its future role in elections is ominous. The public seems increasingly willing to accept and is coming increasingly to demand this projected fabrication of personality in an uncritical frame of mind.

Build-up is a problem for preaching in two ways. First, the preacher himself for the most part lacks any such recommendation or appeal. There have always been preachers who have exerted something of the skills now associated with build-up and the method could doubtless be more widely applied. The trouble here is the disparity between any such projection of himself and the nature of his calling. It serves better for the roving evangelist or the " visiting preacher " whereas, as we shall insist, the real task of preaching is done by those who move constantly among their people and know them and are known by them in situations that make build-up in its usual sense impossible and the deliberate use of it almost a blasphemy. In the second respect, it is a problem for preaching because the hearers have been conditioned to pay little attention to the content, value, or integrity of what is said, and, indeed, to expect what is said to be only a vehicle for the projection of personality. David Riesman, in *The Lonely Crowd,* has this to say of mass persuasion: " The audience situation, moreover, leads to an emphasis not on what the media say in terms of content but on the ' sincerity ' of the presentation. This focus on sincerity, both in popular culture and in politics, leads the audience tolerantly to overlook the incompetence of performance " (p. 211). The net result is a proneness to entertainment, where the critical faculties lie at rest and tend to atrophy — and without an element of criticism there is little application.

A further tendency arises, namely, to accept the role of others as a substitute for one's own action. Again Riesman has pointed to the parallel tendency in the world of mass entertainment: "It may well be, too, that the audience that emphasizes an emotional quality of a performer, such as sincerity, escapes from the need for emotional response to the performance itself " (p. 221). The pulpit has always suffered from this (largely unspoken) demand. The preacher has been expected to be a neighbor, counselor, or rescue worker in a representative capacity, doing what the people often admire but will not, or feel they cannot, do themselves. This representative character is a real function of the minister. Quite obviously, it can be carried too far, since it soon leads to the exclusion of the people from their proper place as followers of Christ. Further build-up in this area would be disastrous in a time when the number of ministers is totally inadequate to the opportunity and the need. What is really under attack here is the gospel principle of practice justifying profession. It seems quite feasible by modern methods of selective presentation to defeat the dictum, " By their fruits ye shall know them." Personalities are accepted on other grounds, and a vast prospect of disillusionment opens up where such personalities have eventually to be put to the test of, let us say, practical politics, economic well-being, or immediate personal relationships, to say nothing of anything resembling a distinctively Christian way of life.

The modern ethos then (here only sketched in its immediate surface manifestations) works against the successful communication of Christian truth and its appropriation as a basis for action in the world. It is one factor in the " loss of audience " and a large one. It helps keep people away from a church that has not received the build-up. Interest in such a religious institution seems an irrelevant, personal hobby. More seriously, it removes the people who *do* come to church as an effective audience even while they are there. It is not entirely that they *will* not hear but that they *can* not. There are clear signs that this is so. The signs are found in the gap, increasingly evident to the discerning, between the thinking of the ministry and the thinking of the laity. The gap becomes more evident the nearer thinking approaches the need to decide about action.

It is to be assumed that the Christian church believes in missions, that is, in carrying the gospel to those who either have never heard it or have been denied the opportunity to practice it in corporate worship and in a Christian society. The churches have come to realize that for the term " missions " (foreign or otherwise) must be substituted the term " the mission of the church." Paganism and ignorance of Christianity are no longer confined to remote and alien lands, nor the need to Christianize society to barbaric tribesmen. There is, however, remarkably little concern or even agreement manifest among the laity. (Exceptions have to be made here. Some ministers have no real concern, and some lay people have an informed zeal; some churches have wonderful records while others, minister and people alike, are concerned only with the religious club life of a few " hereditary Christians.") Somehow, the concern for the spread and application of the evangel has not been communicated to the people, even though without this sense of mission a church can hardly be called in any sense a part of the Church.

The gap is even more clearly marked in the area of the social application of the gospel. Very few denominational conventions or conferences where both ministers and lay people are accredited representatives manage to meet without there developing resistance on the part of the laity to pronouncements, plans, or action in the realm of social reconstruction. The basic assumption that the Christian faith has its own analysis to make and its own direction to take in any matter whatsoever that affects the life of man is not so much as grasped by the majority of laymen. The cry of interference goes up, partly as a result of the history and *raison d'être* of America, which has ingrained in our minds the need for the "separation of church and state." Yet often the issue is not one of the corporate intervention of the churches as such in political, economic, or community affairs, but the expression of a jointly felt point of view identifiable as "Christian." Nor is it that individuals completely resist the actual action, but only that "religion is one thing and politics another." Preaching has failed more signally here than anywhere.

In large measure, the ecumenical movement is a ministerial affair, and even then at top level, because of the gap that exists. The theological grounds for unity felt strongly by the minister have not made an effective contact with or impact on the variety of nontheological factors in the mind and experience of the layman or laywoman. There is, moreover, an impression that ecumenical councils and the like are, for the laymen, the worst offenders in straying from the proper concern of religion into matters of no concern to religion. This failure to implant in lay minds and consciences the true concern of Christianity for the whole of life is the most evident sign of the failure of preaching that there could be. As long as these gaps are not bridged, the non-Christian ethos has an effect more potent than unconcerned or casual preaching can ever deal with. Thus is created the worst gap of all — between an individual " religious " life and all the other involvements of a person with the actual life around him.

So it comes about that even the people who attend church do not really " hear " the sermons. They hear only when the preacher confines himself to purely personal problems immediately felt by the hearer and capable of being ameliorated without bringing the hearer into conflict with the accepted ethos of his society. The failure to create of Christians in a non-Christian society anything distinctive is the clearest sign of the widest gap of all.

Is the situation, in these four aspects, so serious that preaching, having proved to be ineffective, should be abandoned? The answer can be found, not by a direct attack on the problems, but by asking in another way what preaching is as the Christian church has conceived it.

II

OR IS PREACHING ESSENTIAL?

THE SERMON, as distinct from a few specialized forms of Christian propaganda, is an address given by a minister during the course of a service of worship. This has been true since the earliest days when Paul preached in the synagogues of the Jewish Diaspora (see Acts 13:5, 14 ff.; 14:1; etc.), and Justin Martyr (in the second century) recorded the mode of worship with which he was familiar: "And on the day called Sunday there is a meeting in one place of those who live in cities or the country, and the memoirs of the apostles or the writings of the prophets are read as long as time permits. When the reader has finished, the president in a discourse urges and invites [us] to the imitation of these noble things" (*First Apology*, ch. 67). In each case there was clearly a close connection between the reading of Scripture and the spoken discourse. The sermon occupies a much earlier place in Christian worship than, for example, the creed. But preaching is not found to be a part of worship simply because Scripture is read and needs to be expounded. The practice of preaching as a distinctively Christian undertaking is based in the nature of the Christian enterprise as such and arises out of a necessity explicit in the New Testament description of the faith.

The gospel is, by definition, " good news." " Gospel," in English, is derived from the Old English " god spel," — meaning good speech or discourse. It came to be a translation of the Latin *bonus nuntius,* itself a translation of the Greek word discussed below. When " godspel " appeared it had lost its meaning as two separate words and served to designate (*a*) the books of the Evangelists, (*b*) the liturgical reading of a passage from these, and (*c*) the message these contained. " Gospel " is still used in these three ways.

In some sense the gospel is both news and good to hear. News is essentially that which one has to learn and has to wait to hear, even if it does not come entirely unexpectedly and as a complete surprise. If it is known in advance or can be decided and described before it is heard, it is not really " news." This applies whether the news is good or bad. Originally the word " evangel " (*to euangelion*) implied the delivery of a message for which the recipient was willing to reward the bearer. In fact, the term itself meant the reward so paid. In the New Testament the gospel is considered " good " news because the New Testament is written by those who received the message as the means of their deliverance, accepted it and rejoiced in it. Even in its necessary aspect of judgment, the gospel could be good news to them because it showed by this very aspect that God was not indifferent to men and their affairs. It must be remembered that the gospel itself is discriminatory, that it divides and allocates, even if only eschatologically (e.g., Matt. 24:38-41; 25:1-12, 31-46). To those who reject its offer of salvation it can be only the worst possible news — but still news. We are all too prone to read the New Testament as if the news proclaimed were nothing but good to all who hear it. Jesus found, in his own experience, that this was not so, and he had no expectation but that it would effect a division (e.g., Mark 8:38; Luke 12:49-53).

The gospel as described in the New Testament is a proclamation. The word used exhibits both the independence of the message and the initiative of the source from which it originates. It is difficult in English to reproduce the cognate verb and noun relationship involved. Paul, in Gal. 1:11, says, literally, " The evangel that was evangelized by me." This translation indicates that the noun and verb are strictly cognate, forms of the same basic word. The RSV translation of this, "The gospel which was preached by me," obscures this in the interests of good English. The usual word for preach in Greek is *kērussō* and its cognate object is *to kērugma,* neither of which is used in this verse. But it is possible to say in Greek, though it does not make good English, "The gospel that was gospeled by me," and the RSV has combined both. *In short, the method of making known the message is akin to the message itself.* The method must arise out of the content, and the content cannot conceivably be derived from any method just because, as method, it proves itself effective. Here a gap opens up between modern ideas of communication and the essential nature of the task of the Christian communicator of the gospel.

Before we pursue this point, however, we note that what is true of the word " evangel" is true also of "kerygma." The earliest Gospel describes Jesus' work as " preaching the gospel." The words of Mark 1:14 are, literally, " proclaiming the evangel." The verb *kērussō*, here used with " evangel," referred to the work of a herald, whose task it was to proclaim an announcement on behalf of the ruler or ruling body. There is no cognate verb for

" herald," but " proclaim " has its English cognate object in
" proclamation," so that we can say " proclaim a proclamation." In the Greek the corresponding cognate *kērugma*
clearly fits the verb. In modern writings the noun has been
Anglicized in the form " kerygma " and was used by C. H.
Dodd to describe the general pattern of the earliest Christian preaching. In *The Apostolic Preaching and Its Development,* he confines the term " kerygma " to the proclamation of the gospel to the non-Christian world (p. 4).
He distinguishes this from preaching in the more usual
sense where it has come to consist of teaching (*didachē*)
and exhortation (*paraklēsis* — better translated " counsel ")
and a more informal discussion of the Christian life (*ho-
milia*). Our interest in the term " kerygma " at the moment
is that once again the nature of the message is implied in
the method of its being made known, and *the method
arises from the nature of the message and its source.*

We should further note what Paul said in Galatians:
" the gospel gospeled by me is not *according to man.*"
Just because it does not originate with man, man does not
discover it or in any way formulate it. He " receives " it
(Gal. 1:9; as Paul himself did, v.12). The gospel has to be
delivered and it has to be received. So Paul puts it, in I
Cor. 15:1, literally, " The evangel which I evangelized to
you, which also you received." One might say it is like the
mail carrier and the correspondent. The mailman does not
originate the letter that he delivers; nor does the recipient
to whom it is addressed. Behind them both stands the author and sender of the letter.

The postal analogy is not an accurate description of
preaching. There is in the process of preaching another
element to be considered, namely, the character and personality of the preacher himself. The subordination of the

preacher to what is preached is essential for the integrity of the undertaking. The failure to subordinate man to message will result in the message communicated being "according to man" (Gal. 1:11, margin). We see that the New Testament concept of the gospel and its communication is in a sense independent of man. It properly serves the purposes neither of the preacher nor of the recipient, but only God's purpose. It must be "proclaimed" or delivered as news is delivered, coming with an impact different from that which arises from a matter originating in a man or group of men.

At a conference on Christian education, the question was put, "How *do* you teach religion?" This is a largely irrelevant question until further questions have been asked and answered. The method of teaching should depend on the nature of the religion to be taught, and in this respect Christianity differs from all other religions. The gospel cannot be arrived at by solitary meditation or by the process of group discussion. At the very most, all that could be arrived at by these means would be the *need* for such a gospel. The *desirability* of it does not establish it as a thing that exists or that happened. Before the religion of the Gospel can be taught, there is a story to be told and the words ("the Word") that accompanied the events to be made known. Only then can discussion or meditation begin. On rereading Herbert H. Farmer's *The Servant of the Word*, I find that he made the same point in 1941 in relation to the works of Hocking and Barth. He added the striking thought that other religions might lose all their books and followers and yet "substantially the same religion reappear. . . . But were all Christian records and all Christians extirpated, Christianity could not recur again. In its recurrence without a preacher, without a witness, it would flatly contradict all that it had always claimed to be. To put it paradoxically, in happening again it would show that it had never, according to its own definition of itself, happened at all " (p. 19).

This meeting with the Event may come from solitary reading of the Bible, but it has throughout Christian history been chiefly encountered in the corporate hearing of the Scriptures and of comment upon them by a person in some sense representative of the church at large and of the established tradition of Biblical interpretation. There is no private version of the Christian gospel, because it is essentially a corporate possession and its purpose is a corporate one. The personality of the one who communicates the Word is of great importance, chiefly in relating it to the conditions of his hearers, but not with reference to its essential nature.

In short, the Christian gospel is historical in the double sense that it arises from historical events and it becomes active and intelligible only in history (or, in a modern term, " existence "). It testifies to an action of God on the historical plane, which is in no sense conditioned by man as to its origin. This does not make the task of preaching easy, as Emil Brunner observed in *The Scandal of Christianity.* " That is why historical revelation is the great scandal or stumbling block for natural man. Man, filled with his self-love and self-pride, does not want to be uncovered, because he does not want his pride to be infringed upon. To acknowledge historical revelation means to acknowledge that the truth is not in us, that the right relation to God cannot be established from our side; that the breach between God and us is of such a nature that we can do nothing about it" (p. 22).

This fact determines the mode of its presentation and

precludes certain other modes. It makes preaching in its proper sense essential to the Christian faith. In other words, the answer to the question, Should we not give up preaching? is that preaching must not be given up because Christianity is essentially a preached religion — an evangel that has to be evangelized, a proclamation that has to be proclaimed. This is only the beginning, but it is necessary to begin here, and unless there is this beginning, all that follows is irrelevant. This is the primary definition of preaching — that it is the communication of that saving truth which must be communicated or it will not be received. As Paul put it, "Woe to me if I do not preach the gospel" (I Cor. 9:16).

After this has been said, it becomes even more evident that preaching in the twentieth century is a problem. To begin with, "indoctrination" is suspect, and rightly so. We must strive to find if there is some distinction between "preaching," or "communicating the Word," and "indoctrination." Is there a separating line and if so, where does it lie? Further, the essential element in the nature of the gospel that should determine the mode of its propagation is an example of what is designated "mythical" (see the books listed in the bibliography). Any invasion of man's domain from "outside," any intervention into the human order from a divine order, is at once suspect and open to rejection out of hand. To quote Brunner again: "The question of myth divides the spirits. Here is where the decision takes place. For rational thought, not only God's becoming man, but any thought of a God who takes an initiative in the world, is mythology. The argument of myth extends as far as the idea of the personal living God as such. . . . So much can be said: the belief in historical revelation engenders also another conception of God which differs from those held by all mysticism, rationalism or idealist speculation " (pp. 25 f.). This is the whole tenor of the New Testament. To reject its central affirmation of an unconditioned act of God is to reject the Christianity of the New Testament and to substitute something else. It does not help to say that the something else works or is acceptable to the modern mind. It is here that the task of preaching becomes at the outset and remains at every point fundamentally apologetic.

The implication that there is an element of " authority " involved can be dealt with only after we have examined the normal area in which preaching takes place. The indications found in the New Testament that a distinctive form of worship was beginning to emerge are made explicit in the glimpses of the Christian assembly that are found in the scant sources for the first two centuries (explicitly the Didache and Justin Martyr). Thereafter, throughout the centuries and over most of Christendom the *distinctive* form of Christian worship has been the service arising ultimately from the Last Supper as recorded in the Gospels and the First Letter to the Corinthians. Its roots are in all probability to be found in the domestic religious observances of the Jewish home. For our purpose it matters little whether this service is now called the Lord's Supper, the Holy Mysteries, the Holy Ordinance, the Eucharist, the Mass, or the Holy Communion, or any other name. Each of these terms has its peculiar connotations and indicates a different emphasis. In connection with the variations of the rite, the sermon has waxed and waned and sometimes disappeared.

The other general form of Christian worship may best be described as the ministry of the Word. This is based more distinctly on the synagogue form of worship than on the home or Temple observances of the Jews. Although its great development has come with the Reformation emphasis on the Bible, the form was by no means new in the sixteenth century. It had been in use for centuries (even if in somewhat truncated form) in the daily offices of the monastery and of the secular clergy. It has always appeared in the sacramental rite as the " proanaphora " or " mass of the catechumens " or the " antecommunion." In the daily offices there was, as a rule, no sermon. This was reserved for the gathering of the Lord's people on the Lord's Day, when the principal service was the Mass, until the Reformation began the process of displacement. Yet, whether there was a sermon or whether, because of the ignorance of priests or a magical emphasis on the Sacrament, it was neglected, the element of the ministry of the Word, in which the sermon found its natural place, was invariably present in some form. It was usually preliminary to the more distinctly sacramental rite and served as an introduction to it. The significance of this is worth a little consideration.

The present trend of revived liturgical interest and re-evaluation in all the churches has been toward the recovery of the essential interrelation of Word and Sacrament. For the liturgical churches this means a renewed emphasis on the ministry of the Word; for the nonliturgical churches, on re-exploration of the possibility of making the Lord's Supper a more frequent service. As A. Allan McArthur has pointed out, the beadle in the Church of Scotland carries the Bible to the pulpit each Sunday, thus marking the centrality of the Word. On Communion Sundays the bread and wine are likewise brought in by the elders. He observes: " These two significant actions make visible the two distinct parts of the public worship of God, namely, the ministry of the Word of God and the celebration of the Sacrament. . . . It is the Word and Sacrament which together constitute the normative liturgy . . . the proclamation of the divine will in the Word and the assurance of the divine presence in the Sacrament." (*The Christian Year and Lectionary Reform*, p. 15. It may be noted here that the allocation of will to Word and presence to Sacrament is not the most satisfying statement of the case.) R. E. C. Browne has well stated the dual function of the ministry: "We do not say that the ministry of the Word is more important than the ministry of the Sacrament or that the ministry of the Sacrament is more important than the ministry of the Word. The two ministries are complementary, rather, two expressions of one ministry" (*The Ministry of the Word*, p. 117).

The same combination may be seen in the magnificent new Communion service of the still young Church of South India. Here there are three major divisions to the service: the Preparation, the Ministry of the Word of God, and the Breaking of Bread. Whether we take this or any other representative form of service that includes the use of Scripture and the Lord's Supper in a reformed liturgy, we find basically the same pattern. It is found alike in the *Book of Common Order of the Church of Scotland* (where an intercession, however, comes in the longer form between the optional creed and the sermon), in *The Book of Common Prayer*, in the Lutheran liturgies, and receives its stress in *An Experimental Liturgy*, published in the series, Ecumenical Studies in Worship, No. 3. The pattern is derived from the most ancient of the fully developed liturgies, and in it the sermon is found in close association with the reading of Scripture. The more usual Sunday-by-Sunday service of the Reformed churches goes behind this development to approximate more closely the synagogue form. In this " service of worship " the sermon has a prominent place, and to this we shall return below. We note here the fairly consistent place the sermon holds in the more complete or " double " form in order to consider its relation with what comes before and after, both in relation with the ministry of the Word and the sacrament of the Lord's Table.

In the usual form there is introductory prayer and sometimes an act of praise, followed by a variable collect connected with the season of the year and in some measure summing up the meaning of the Scripture that is to follow. At this point comes the reading of the Bible in the form of short pericopes. These may consist of one from the Old Testament, one from the New Testament outside the Gospels (" the Epistle "), and a concluding one from the Four Gospels — or of the latter two, omitting the Old Testament selection. It is at this point that the sermon comes either preceding or following the recitation of one of the historic creeds. This is a very ancient pattern. In Justin Martyr, the address appears to have been immediately related to the reading and served as a commentary on it. In *The Book of Common Prayer* of the Anglican churches, this is the only place at which a sermon is provided for, confirming the impression that the Holy Communion, with its preliminary ministry of the Word, was intended to be the principal service for Sundays when all the people of Christ gathered together. Nothing could more strikingly indicate the significant place the sermon was intended to hold (even if often honored in the breach by a Communion without a sermon or a sermon without Communion).

Clearly the placing of the sermon in this position, with its long tradition of being so placed, indicates the intention. The purpose of the sermon is to be construed from its position, namely, it is to expound, clarify, and apply the Christian faith as it arises out of and rests back upon the Scriptures. Whether the creed precedes or follows the sermon, this further indicates that it is the Christian faith that is being expounded but as that faith, traditionally summed up in the historic symbols, finds its ultimate authority in the Word of God. Even where the creeds are not used (and they are not the most ancient part of the service), the Word of God is normally expounded in keeping with the theological development that represents the tradition of the preacher's own branch of the church. The Scriptures themselves (in particular, the Gospels) are increasingly recognized to be theological statements and interpretations rather than directly transcribed " pure " history. If we take this very ancient arrangement to be the guide, we should then say that the sermon is intended to be *theological* and *Scriptural*. In what sense it may or should be either of these we must examine more fully.

Meanwhile, we note that in the traditional liturgies the sermon is normally followed by the action of the sacramental rite, starting with an offertory in some form and accompanied, as a rule, by an offering of intercession. Beyond this lies the action of setting apart the bread and wine, held in a framework of thanksgiving and coming to a climax in the reception by the worshipers of the sacramental means of Communion. This is not the only kind of action involved, however, for underlying the " liturgical action " and arising out of it is the expectation that the worshipers will extend the action of the church into the world as action in society. This is sometimes given explicit expression, but in any case it is involved in the consecration of the worshipers to their Lord, who offered himself for the whole world.

The significance of liturgical action following upon the preaching of the sermon is that the sermon itself gains a function in relation to it. The sermon is expected to be, in a sense, *liturgical*. This does not mean that it need be a discussion of liturgical procedure (though on occasions this may helpfully find justification and elucidation in a sermon), but that it should aim to bring the liturgical action into relation to the faith derived from Scripture and to give the whole relevance to a particular people at a particular time in connection with some particular application of that common faith. It should be stressed that worship has its purely " objective " aspect — it exists to glorify God, and the sermon must not distract from this purpose but reinforce this outgoing action.

It is also possible to suggest that the sermon should likewise point forward to the other type of action, which should result from the act of worship itself. Properly designed and carried out, the worship should have some relevance to the worshipers' life in the world. It is preparation for the expression of the Christian life in the affairs of men. The reality and effectiveness of the worship as well as of the sermon is to be judged by its ability to effect this connection and result. The liturgical action, including the sermon within itself, should therefore be a means of giving renewed or even new expression to some aspect of the Biblical faith as a " formal " anticipation of some application outside the gathering when those assembled disperse to take up their work and relationships in their " real " life. Therefore, the sermon would appear to be intended to be *pastoral* in the fullest and most proper sense of that word.

Though what has been said is derived from the liturgical forms of worship, it applies with no less force to nonliturgical forms. "The service of the Word" in the common worship of nonliturgical churches normally places the sermon in a more climactic position. It is prepared for by a pattern of worship that usually includes an invocation or call to worship, a responsive reading (generally from Scripture), a reading of the Bible, and a pastoral prayer (which may embody traditional elements of worship — thanksgiving, praise, confession, intercession). The whole is customarily interspersed with congregational hymns, choir anthems, and organ music. In a well-planned service the sermon is then integrated into the whole (or the whole is integrated into the sermon theme), which finds its climax in the preaching. The sermon, in turn, may be followed by an offering, on occasion by the Lord's Supper, but normally the climactic point is the sermon itself. There is a lot to be said for this when the sermon is really integrated with the rest of the service. In the words of John Knox, " Unless we conceive of preaching as being itself an act of worship, we miss what is most essential in it and what distinguishes it most radically from other kinds of teaching, religious or secular " (*The Integrity of Preaching*, p. 76). The climactic point is also the place the sermon occupies in the full liturgical service. In the nonliturgical, nonsacramental service, however, it can more readily be directly pointed toward the functioning of Christians in the world. What is lacking is any particular opportunity to give expression to the sermon theme in the service itself, any major acts of worship transitional to action in the world.

It would not be correct to say that in such a service the sacramental element is entirely lacking. A sacrament is usually understood to involve the effective use of some out-

ward sign or symbol. While words are not "material" in
the physical sense, they are in a very real sense the product
of physical effort and are the "outward" expression of un-
seen things. They are intangible but yet in fact "sensory."
They are also the most widely used and effective of modern symbols. (On this whole matter, see F. W. Dillistone,
Christianity and Symbolism.) Quite apart from the oc-
currence of Baptism or the Supper of the Lord, the Word
of God read and proclaimed is therefore sacramental in a
real sense. In the West we are inclined to take too subjective a view of the operation of the Word of God. We do
not so fully as our Continental brethren grasp the objective reality and functional power of the Word itself. The
means used in the ministry of the Word are as objective as
the water of Baptism or the bread and wine of the Communion. They are effective means of effecting contact
between people at their deepest level, whether the Word is
written or spoken. They are a vehicle, a symbol, which
gives effect to that which it indicates, and as such they
have a sacramental function. Words are the means of
transmission of the Word of God, that central and revealing message which the Bible as a book transmits. Further,
the most sublime statement of the incarnation of the Son
of God is given in the statement, "The Word became
flesh."

Goethe detected that if the first verse of John's Gospel
applied only to words as usually conceived, something
was lacking. He accordingly suggested that thought might
be compelled to move forward from "In the beginning
was the Word," thus: "*Im Anfang war das Wort!* . . .
Im Anfang war der Sinn. . . . *Im Anfang war die Kraft.*
. . . *Im Anfang war die Tat!*" When he ends with "In
the beginning was the Deed" (or Act), he has grasped the

meaning that, while it does not displace the term " Word," it must, when it is applied to God embrace also the action that a word from God effects. It was put, long before Goethe's *Faust,* by Ben Sira: " By the words of the Lord his works are done " (Ecclus. 42:15). The unfailing purpose of God's Word was also stated in Isa. 55:10-11 (RSV):

" For as the rain and the snow come down from heaven,
    and return not thither but water the earth,
making it bring forth and sprout,
    giving seed to the sower and bread to the eater,
so shall my word be that goes forth from my mouth;
    it shall not return to me empty,
but *it shall accomplish that which I purpose,*
    and prosper in the thing for which I sent it."

Therefore, in the ministration of the Word, which uses words to express the Word of God, we are coming into contact with the Word of God himself. That is to say, sacramentally conceived, there is a presence of Christ in the ministry of the Word as well as in the ministry of the sacraments, a presence at least as real and as demanding. It is as real an encounter with the Lord of the church as any other act. It may, indeed, on occasion be more explicitly so. In prayer it may be all too easy to be preoccupied with personal or human needs, and the same may be said of praise (except when it is in the words of Scripture), but the reading of the Word of God has an objectiveness and independence that does not conform itself to our preferences. It confronts us, demanding and inviting, on its own terms. Even the sacramental rites of the Christian church, which have been subject to manipulation by human hands in human interests, are rites that use and need to use words for their completeness (or even "validity"). That the words of the traditional rites may not be chosen by whim or at random is the theme of all liturgical history. This insistence is found originally in the concern of Paul to deliver (*paredōka*) what he had received (*parelabon*) of the Lord (I Cor. 11:23-25), and of the Synoptic Gospels to record the etiological stories of the Last Supper. The divorce of the Word of God from the sacraments makes the sacraments themselves less intelligible, less likely to involve the participants in relevant action in relation to them. It was this which the Reformation recovered when the worship of the church was put into the vernacular and the reading of consecutive passages of Scripture was restored to both the offices and the people's liturgy.

This sense of the impact of the Word of God has been a major note in the revival of relevant theology in modern times and can conveniently be associated with the name of Karl Barth. His book *The Word of God and the Word of Man,* dealing with the " strange new world within the Bible " as it relates to the task of preaching in the twentieth century, clearly expresses the objective power of the Word of God.

To whatever extent, then, this is true, there arise certain problems for preaching, problems that in themselves are problems of recovery of the answer from which the problems arise. That is to say, the problems arise from the answer that preaching finds its real meaning and power in the objective character of the Word of God. The problems concern the relation of worship and of the preacher to the task of the ministry of the Word. At first sight, the liturgical churches would seem to have solved one part of the problem in that the subjective element provided by the preacher's choice of passages of the Bible to read has been largely eliminated. This is a matter to which we shall turn later. Another element in the problem is, granted that the preacher has some sense of the authority of the Word with which he deals, how is he to communicate this to the congregation and how is he to bridge the gap between the largely different worlds of the Bible and the modern hearer? Still more urgently, the original question, Why preach at all? remains to be answered.

The claim of Christian preaching is, in essence, the claim of the Bible, namely, to disclose an activity of God toward man that is independent of man's initiative. It is a misconception of Christianity's place among the religions of the world to suppose that the Christian gospel is or could be produced by human cogitation. The essence of the Biblical revelation is that it is a revelation, and a revelation primarily through action taken by the initiative of God. Yet the very possibility of a revelation is denied by modern man. It is this Biblical Word, as personal activity, virtually a " hypostasis," which in Christ became flesh and lived as man and died a human death and rose again as " Son of God in power" (Rom. 1:4). In this view of the Bible as the Word of God (more properly, of the Word of God operative through the Bible), the basis for preaching is discovered in its necessity and in the first suggestion of its authority.

Our brief discussion of the place of the sermon in the framework of worship suggested that it is an undertaking integral to the Christian fellowship gathered together as " church." Is it, then, in the assembly rather than, or as well as, in the activity of the Word of God that the authority of preaching is found? Every attempt to arrive at a fixed and satisfactory definition of the source of authority meets with qualification. There is always a "but." Apostolic authority was doomed to disappear when the "apostles" disappeared. The undivided church claimed the title "apostolic" and found the locus of authority in the "apostolic succession" of bishops. As schism developed, there arose conflicting claims of "catholicity," and the rise of Protestant churches further complicated the matter. By this time the discovery of the breakdown of real authority in the divided church led the Protestant churches to appeal to the Bible as the final source. Here a qualification entered at first when the question was asked, Whose interpretation of the Bible? and again when the question became, In what sense is the Bible the Word of God?

It becomes apparent that a claim to authority that must be qualified (even where it is imposed "by authority") can be an authority only where it is accepted as such. In spite of qualification and a recognition that authority must in some sense be qualified, there *is* real meaning to the phrases "authority of the church" and "authority of the Bible." There is real meaning also to a joint authority of church and Bible in which the church interprets the Bible and the Bible stands in judgment on the church. No discussion of the source or nature of authority in religion can realistically evade the share played in the determination of the issue by the *acceptance* of authority. At the highest level, this has been conceived as the *testimonium Spiritus Sancti internum* (inner testimony of the Holy Spirit.) This has sometimes meant in practice nothing more than the emotional predilections of the hearers, but can better be thought of as the testing of claims by experience when such experience is itself believed to be under the influence of the Spirit of God.

There is no intention to pursue the matter here. It is mentioned because preaching as here understood involves *a joint operation of the Bible, the church, and the hearer.* Whether we consider so-called Biblical preaching or liturgical preaching, all three are involved. In the term "Biblical preaching," the role of the church is less conspicuously emphasized; in "liturgical preaching" it is more so. The Biblical preacher may claim complete freedom to interpret the Scriptures, and yet the formation of the Bible cannot be thought of apart from the activity of the Judaeo-Christian church. Liturgical preaching is more dependent on a church for the selection of the Biblical material to be interpreted, but can scarcely control the preacher in his interpretation unless the sole basis of authority is in fact the church itself. In any case, the hearer is involved in acceptance of the authority claimed or implied. When acceptance is fully operative, the authority is authoritative.

Beyond this lies the claim of the gospel itself to an authority that must control the preacher. There will be a demand that the gospel be mediated not only in the preacher's discourse but through the preacher himself (Phillips Brooks's element of "personality"). Ideally, the authority will be recognized to be the gospel, mediated through the preacher's personality from the Bible within the church, when it proves itself effective in the hearers, because it comes to them as a revelation, as "news" that brings good. Put in this rather matter-of-fact way (which I would contend reflects the actual situation, whatever the theological determination of the question might be), certain things are involved for our discussion of the task of preaching.

First, the preacher is not free to share with his congregation any thoughts whatever that happen to interest him at the moment. His very position precludes this. The gathering of the congregation within the church and the appointment of the preacher as their minister, if not his delegation by a wider body of the church, suggest at once that his task is to deliver what he has *received* and not what he has concocted. If he stands in a pulpit and wears robes of ministerial office, the point is all the more obvious. He cannot stand in the pulpit, garbed as an official representative of his church, and take advantage of his position to impose upon the silent congregation his own ideas. Nor is he really even free to choose to speak on any subject that happens to have aroused his passing or persistent interest. He must in some way justify what he presents as relevant to the undertaking in which he and his congregation are involved — unless, in fact, the whole procedure is a matter simply of a Sunday morning's entertainment, and of no more moment than any other entertainment. The point is driven home by the silence of the congregation. Their willingness to accept topic and presentation in itself implies the acceptance of some kind of authority.

The second point is that the decay of Biblical and liturgical preaching have made ambiguous the position both of preacher and preached-to. The virtual disappearance of the " text " is a symptom. There are many good reasons for not using a text, and such reasons may actually be dictated by the requirements of truly Biblical preaching. But the absence of a text or of a passage of Scripture to be expounded calls in question the whole proceeding. Unless the preacher is communicating the message of the Bible or is speaking of the faith of the church, what is he doing in the pulpit? He may perhaps be either entertaining the audience with ideas interesting in themselves, or giving expression publicly to thoughts that the community approves and likes to hear stated well — better than the average person could state them. In either case, the question arises, Why the Christian minister? Could not anyone else at all do that? What is he doing that the scoutmaster, or school principal, or chairman of the service club, could not do as well, perhaps better? More cogent still, would not a discussion group serve better the corporate expression of the group and be more effective in terms of group dynamics? So that once again we come to the question of the *inherent* necessity of the gospel to be preached and find that it is an element in the very function of the preacher in the church.

The preacher in his pulpit before the assembly is there to preach the gospel as that which must be preached and to guide in its application as a way of life. To this end the true preacher has been ordained and set apart, and for this reason a true church has gathered to be ministered to. If this is correct, the preacher is under some obligation to seek beyond his own interests for his message. If he wishes to discuss his own ideas, he should make it clear that this is what he is doing by divesting himself of official robes, by leaving the pulpit, and by permitting his audience to participate in the discussion. If it is as a voice of the community that he functions, then all the more certainly he should moderate a forum. If he ascends a pulpit and stands garbed in the robes of authority, he is no longer at liberty to do other than the church intends its ministers to do, or to present anything other than the gospel (in its broadest sense) in the mode appropriate to the gospel.

The presentation of the gospel in its proper mode is really our subject — that is to say, its *effective* presentation, so that its authority depends on no externals but on an actual encounter between God and man, in which encounter the preacher is, by the mercy of God, permitted a part.

As soon as this is said, however, we are back at the other point, the point of apologetic. The nearer the preacher is to performing the task that inheres in the nature of the gospel itself, the farther he is from the people who sit before him at the present time. The element that has been called " mythical " becomes the more evident the nearer the preacher comes to the New Testament conception of the gospel. Therefore, both from the nature of New Testament Christianity and from the mode of presentation inherent in the evangel to be evangelized or the proclamation to be proclaimed, there arises the problem of bridging the gap between the Biblical message and the modern hearer. On the one side lies the matter of an authority consonant with the message, and to this we shall first turn. On the other side lies the matter of securing its acceptance, and to this we can return only when we have examined the basic matter to be presented.

III

THE ORDERING
OF BIBLICAL PREACHING

THERE CAN be no certainty that the gospel is being presented by the preacher unless there is some contact with the Scriptures and the church at large, both in space and time, to provide the context of interpretation. Mere contact with the Scriptures, however, does not guarantee this certainty. If the connection is left entirely to the discretion of the preacher, the congregation becomes dependent on the preacher rather than on the Bible. This dependence will then be good or bad according to whether the preacher is well equipped and has a proper understanding of his task.

The following qualifications at least would be necessary to provide real assurance:

1. A knowledge of the Scriptures as a whole, such as would enable him always to have in mind relevant passages with an awareness of their relationship to each other;

2. An ability to organize and arrange the Scriptures for use in a cycle that would afford the congregation a full and rounded periodic presentation of the gospel and its application to a way of life;

3. A grasp of the problems presented by modern Biblical study and the skill to present the positive contribution it offers;

4. Freedom from preoccupation with a particular area or application of the gospel and willingness to present aspects of the Biblical *Heilsgeschichte* (story of salvation) with which he feels less congenial but which are necessary to a fully rounded presentation; and

5. An awareness of contemporary pastoral needs that, brought to the analysis of the Biblical material, would produce a Christian understanding of those problems and prepare the way for an "evangelical" and "existential" solution. This is to ask too much of the preacher.

Yet, on the other hand, too much is asked of the listener. Let us look at it from his point of view. He is a man, let us say, who through the previous week has been troubled by the almost insuperable difficulty of squaring modern business methods with his Christian profession and what he knows of the demands of God's laws. He is caught in the inflationary spiral and has been disturbed by problems of maintaining the mortgage payments and providing future security and education for his family out of a budget already strained. He has been aware of subconscious questionings about his place in the scheme of things and of his own identity. Hovering over all is the shadow of atomic warfare and what his position will be if hostilities commence. In addition, he has struggled with Sunday lethargy and made a real effort to subdue the household confusion, so that he and his family have been able to come to church.

This man rather naturally expects that he will be offered some help related to these problems. Is the work he is engaged in and its problems, his struggle to maintain a standard of living, his introspective musing in any way illuminated by the gospel of Christ? Can he find any reassurance, any new direction or clue to understanding?

In this situation, having made this effort, he is hardly to be satisfied by a debate about the author of the passage of Scripture, a discussion of the liturgical history of the service, the chronological problem involved in a chapter of Biblical history, or by the minister's account of a conference he has attended. Still less will his need be met by a sermon that is yet another fulmination on the preacher's pet peeve or personal angle, and least of all by a sermon scolding people for not coming to church or not engaging in some other " religious " activity — which he, for one, might be prepared to do if his interest were aroused or some help promised by continued attendance and commitment.

Such a person and such sermons are not rare but are known to most of us. This man and his situation need to be kept in mind in discussing any orderly plan of Scriptural preaching because any scheme designed to save the minister from himself should be designed to save him for the actual people he serves. They are easily lost sight of in discussing the " archaeology " of seasons and lections.

The men and women in the congregation can be protected from the limitations and idiosyncrasies of the preacher by an orderly and cyclical plan that imposes upon the preacher some element of authority, control, or guidance, but is not in itself a strait jacket. The fear of killing the preacher's freedom and spontaneity has been greatly exaggerated. Where spontaneity exists (as a welcome discovery in place of the use of canned material), it is too hardy and vigorous to be thus easily destroyed. As I think we shall see, freedom will rather be stimulated and directed. A proper scheme will provide ample room for originality, but only if the preacher is conversant with the scheme as a whole and himself does some planning in relating the provided material to his own experience, to conditions of time and place, to the known needs of his people, and to an annual round treated in the consciousness of other years to come.

An ordered scheme is not, in itself, a guarantee. Even where a plan of liturgical preaching is provided for and clearly available for preliminary planning, it is all too possible to find preachers who deal on a random Sunday with a topic that is the outstanding theme for a day yet to come (or even just past). It is even possible to find a man preaching this Sunday on a theme that is markedly the core of the next Sunday's readings. This is plainly lack of self-discipline, even if it comes primarily from lack of attention imposed by the pressure of other duties. If preaching is to recover its place, there must be some better distribution of attention. The late Dean George Hodges, when he was minister of a large church in Pittsburgh, was right, in essence, when he claimed part of his working week as a parish minister for the people as a whole. He meant that some hours should be protected against individual conferences and group meetings in order that they might be used to prepare not only sermons but the preacher for dealing with his people as a congregation and over a period of time. This is not to endorse the writing of a whole batch of sermons at one time (for example, on a summer vacation) because the immediacy of pastoral contact and contemporary event is absent. The planning of a rounded scheme of preaching is an obligation that cannot be shirked. The opportunity within it of being always relevant is neither impossible nor inconsistent.

The value of any such scheme is a matter for demonstration rather than for argument. The revived and growing interest in liturgical preaching is everywhere evident.

The so-called liturgical revival is incomplete (I would say, unrealistic) without it. The nonliturgical churches have shown a growing interest in an ecclesiastical year with some plan of using Biblical material and, presumably, with an expectation of preaching based upon it. The most notable indication of this is A. Allan McArthur's invaluable book, *The Evolution of the Christian Year,* followed by his specific suggestions in *The Christian Year and Lectionary Reform.* The Episcopal Church has produced a symposium, *Preaching the Christian Year,* in addition to a steady restudying of its lectional material, and in the Church of England, R. H. Fuller has produced *What Is Liturgical Preaching?* There are Roman Catholic and Lutheran expositions of the themes provided in their respective " propers " for the Mass and Holy Communion. The series of short books being produced under the title Ecumenical Studies in Worship has a direct bearing on the subject and is a symptom of the widespread interest. The scrolls discovered at Qumrân have provided abundant material to compel the restudy of Jewish, Orthodox, and sectarian calendars as a background. (See J. T. Milik, *Ten Years of Discovery in the Wilderness of Judaea,* Studies in Biblical Theology, No. 26, pp. 107 ff.)

Perhaps the term " liturgical preaching " is an unfortunate one. It suggests that the discussion must be confined to preaching in liturgically ordered services or in churches that have a fixed liturgy. This is not necessarily the case. An annual, biennial, or even triennial scheme of reading the Scriptures in worship and preaching upon them is not impossible; nor is it by any means unknown in nonliturgical circles. Such a scheme need not occupy *every* Sunday. It can be concerned with seasonal cycles, fixing some Sundays and leaving others free. Neither does the term confine the preaching to a discussion of the liturgy, even if readings from the Bible are properly thought of as part of the liturgy. We have said that sermons should be liturgical, but this applied to their organic relation to the service whether that is liturgical in the strict sense of the word or not. An always present danger in the term is that it tends to focus attention on the mechanics rather than on the people involved, the preacher and his hearers. In other words, it concentrates on the term "liturgical" rather than on the term "preaching." Even the expression "preaching the Christian year" tends to place emphasis on the means rather than on the aim and must be read as shorthand for "Preaching to the congregation the classic and evangelical themes as arranged for the observance of a Christian year." The term "Biblical preaching" is not an exact substitute and will be dealt with later.

The fact that the Christian or ecclesiastical year can be mentioned suggests a fairly general understanding of the basic arrangement. It has, of course, been a matter of age-long tradition, and we are now in a better position to review the usual ordering and understand its nature. At many points the traditional plan is far from being mandatory — or even intelligible. It is obviously subject to review in the light of modern Biblical knowledge. It is fixed more by traditional inertia than by any inherent necessity. It has no claim to be a Procrustean bed into which all ecclesiastical calendars, plans of worship, and preaching need to be squeezed. The value of its major points of transition and concentration derives partly from the length of the tradition associated with them and partly from the unity of attention that a very large part of Christendom has formed the habit of paying to them.

There is actually only one fixed point. The inseparable

event, crucifixion-resurrection, is unassailably linked with an annually recurring natural phenomenon, the full moon of barley harvest in ancient Palestine, which determined the date of Passover and therefore determines the date of Easter. On this depends Good Friday. The continued observance of Easter as the Christian Pascha on the properly determined date not only provides the whole scheme with a pivot but in itself testifies to the historical nature of the Christian faith. Proposals arbitrarily to fix the date of Easter have the strength of avoiding confusion for those who plan sales campaigns and vacations. They have the decided weakness of loosening the one vital link with historical circumstances and would represent a further surrender to secularism.

The other generally accepted fixed point is Christmas, but the celebration of the Nativity of our Lord on December 25 is an arbitrary date, adjusted originally to a non-Christian Roman holiday and soon associated with the winter solstice in the northern hemisphere. The date has never been accepted by the Armenian Church. Their Nativity feast is on January 6, and this has become a secondary Christmas (or extended " octave ") in the West, the Twelfth-night of Shakespeare's time. In view of the extreme secularization of Christmas in Western lands, there is a great deal to be said for moving it or even abandoning it, but the tradition has become so fixed and about it have clustered so many folkways that the suggestion has an element of the fantastic. The saving possibility here, which needs to be more fully exploited by the churches, is to begin the Christmas celebration on Christmas Day or its eve and continue it for a number of days thereafter (for the standard octave, including at least one Sunday). By this time the commercial and advertising interests have ceased their exploitation of Christmas themes and tunes and turned to other matters, leaving the churches free to concentrate on the distinctively Christian aspects and their theological application.

Concerning these two foci of the year, two things need to be said. First, it will be noted that the two points, Easter and Christmas, in the northern hemisphere, involve a close tie with the natural seasons. Easter is roughly associated with the sun's crossing of the equator on its return north, effecting the reawakening of natural life and the activity of seed-sowing. This affords an obvious parable of the new life brought by the resurrection of Christ but has somewhat unfortunate connotations with pagan myths. Christmas hails the turning of the sun from its lowest southern point and easily associates itself with the birth of the Light of the World. Again the mythological connotations could be embarrassing for sophomoric minds. Obviously, these connections fail outside the northern hemisphere. This means that either the ecclesiastical calendar must be changed to conform to nature or that southern-hemisphere and equatorial Christians are free to concentrate on the religious significance of the dates with less confusion with folkways and pagan mythology.

The second point is that the Christian and theological application of the celebrations is paramount, and the festivals become Christian festivals only as they are increasingly differentiated in essence from the commercial exploitation, nature-mythology, and paganized jollification of secular society. It is not hard to see why the Puritans (quite apart from the associations of Mariolatry) abandoned the celebration of Christmas. The redemption of the festival is the better if exceedingly harder way.

The point at issue, however, resolves itself into a discus-

sion whether the ecclesiastical calendar is intended to celebrate step by step the life of Jesus or whether it celebrates
point by point the great doctrines of the Christian faith.
The fact that normally Christmas is the first great occasion (the anticipation of which has all but obliterated Advent) gives the initial impression that the church is em-
barking upon an annual rehearsal of the events in the life
of Christ. Traces of this are seen in the cluster of lesser
celebrations tied to the date of Christmas — the Circumcision of Christ (Jan. 1), the Epiphany (Jan. 6), the
Presentation of Christ in the Temple (medieval "Purifica-
tion," Feb. 2), and the Annunciation to Mary (March 25),
which looks forward to another Christmas to come. Attached to Easter is the solemnity of Good Friday, the institution of the Lord's Supper on the day previous, and
the entry into Jerusalem on Palm Sunday. Good Friday at
least marks a historical connection. As far as the original
event is concerned, Easter depends upon that Friday, but
in liturgical history the observance of Good Friday arose
out of the keeping of the Christian Pascha. Modern studies
tend to raise questions about Maundy Thursday and
Palm Sunday. The major festivals that succeed Easter
(Whitsunday fifty days later and Ascension ten days before it) have a basis in the uncritical reading of The Acts
of the Apostles and in the survival of the fiftieth-day celebration of the Jews, baptized as a Christian feast. In any
case, they deal with events that are not historical in the
same sense as the crucifixion is historical. They have a
vital meaning for Christian faith and, like Easter itself,
an essential connection with history, but their prime significance lies in the realm of Christian experience and its
theological elucidation.

Problems begin to multiply as soon as a real attempt is

made to use the traditional seasons between Christmas and Easter as steps in the life of Christ. The beginning of Lent has come to be associated with Jesus' temptation in the wilderness as the inauguration of a forty-day period of self-discipline. In the modern world and even in the ordinary church, it is too long for a concentrated program and too short for a real review of Christ's ministry. Moreover, the ancient day for noting the baptism of Jesus (which in the Synoptic Gospels is directly associated with the temptation at the beginning of the ministry) is the Epiphany itself. It had this purpose before East and West exchanged festivals and the Magi took over the Western Epiphany. Anyone who has seriously tried to make chronological sense of the Circumcision followed by the Epiphany, followed by the Presentation, realizes how unreal the arrangement is if it is meant to be a historical rehearsal.

The study of traditional attempts to deal with these problems, reflected in set prayers and readings, is full of interest but hardly of vital importance to the real issue. The real problem is the planning of an orderly review of the essentials of the gospel revelation to be presented in worship and illuminated by preaching in the contemporary world. In so far as the essentials are summed up in the historic creeds, a cycle might well be constructed upon the basis of the " moments " of revelation there supplied. Dr. McArthur says, " A lectionary based upon this conception has never been erected " (*The Christian Year*, p. 66 — his " Peterhead Lectionary " attempts it). He finds the need to re-establish orderly reading of the Bible in the dangers that arise from subjective choices as a basis for sermons. Even where a whole course is planned, " subjectivism remains, and in the proclamation of the Word of

God the congregation is not led *from landmark to land-mark in the great objective stream of Christian doctrine* " (p. 28, my italics). Modern understanding of the New Testament really requires that the " biographical" sequence should give place to a " doctrinal" sequence.

The answer to the dilemma that places the life of Christ over against a development of doctrinal occasions is not the exclusion of the one in favor of the other but a combination in which they are held in tension. The attempt to use a chronological basis is doomed to confusion by the passing of the uncritical acceptance of a linear co-ordination of the four Gospels. The stress upon the creedal points of emphasis is still valid but, divorced from a recognition that real events are celebrated (which did happen in a temporal series), surrenders too readily to the increasingly docetic tendency of some aspects of modern theology. To say it does not matter whether we can know anything of the history, works, words, and person of Jesus is to undermine the essential Christian faith in favor of a doctrinal abstraction and to surrender to the confusion of needs arising from present existence. The tension involved in the traditional calendar between historical series and creedal affirmation is of the essence of Christianity. The celebration of a church year with periodic fixed points (which need be very few) is a rehearsal of the major tenets of the traditional creedal symbols (Apostles' and Nicene) and, like them, makes doctrinal points that are conditioned by actual historical events experienced and interpreted by the primitive church.

By way of demonstration rather than of argument, the following attempt is made to display the major Christian seasons as generally accepted in such manner as to suggest themes for preaching and to show how at certain points generalization must be made in order to avoid unnecessary restriction to an arbitrary scheme.

Advent. This is a solemn preparation for the whole church year in general and for Christmas in particular, embracing four Sundays. It introduces the principle of *alternation* — festivals prepared for by a period of self-examination, corporate repentance, and discipline, followed by a festival of rejoicing extended for a corresponding or longer period. Conventionally the Advent theme was eschatological. It came to revolve around a discussion of " the last things " — death, judgment, hell, and heaven. This confines the plan to a limited sense of the term " eschatological." The opposite extreme swings the season over to a preparation for Christmas. The Reformers, in arranging *The Book of Common Prayer,* produced no such scheme. They tried to relate the season both to the historical coming of Christ and to the expectation of his coming again.

The suggestion to be made here is that the season should concern itself with *God's relation to history.* This embraces the preparation of the world in Old Testament history and prophecy for the coming of the Messiah and gives weight to the eventual goal of history and the destiny of man as revealed in the New Testament. The former interest can be used in advance and come to a climax or summation in Advent, and the latter finds its counterpart or echo in the celebration of the ascension (see below). Within this broad theme there is opportunity for annual variation by the use of " series " of sermons that may cover in turn many of the traditional topics and provide a fit preparation for the true understanding of the doctrine of the incarnation, or God as historical Person.

Christmas. The problem of Christmas for the preacher

is what has been aptly called "the domestication of the incarnation." The vexatious question of myth and history is very much involved here. Yet the preacher would be ill-advised to discard the "folk" character of the story. The real issue is whether the occasion is a celebration of the birthday of Jesus (date and day unknown) or of the Christian affirmation of the becoming-man of the Son of God. It would be highly advisable to make all chosen readings serve to underline the theological theme. It is, itself, in the modern sense of the word, mythological, and this may as well be faced on the first major feast day. It is easier to approach the symbolical details of the Nativity story from this point of view than to arrive at the doctrine from a domesticated and factual treatment of the manger, shepherds, and Wise Men (who intrude themselves by popular demand).

The incarnation in the New Testament, especially as it concerns itself with the virgin birth (more properly, virgin conception), is secondary to the proclamation of the crucified and risen Lord and derives therefrom. The words T. S. Eliot supplied for Thomas à Becket's Christmas sermon in his play *Murder in the Cathedral* are a good clue to the importance of holding the teaching of the Nativity in close connection with the cross:

Dear children of God, my sermon this morning will be a very short one. I wish only that you should ponder and meditate the deep meaning and mystery of our masses of Christmas Day. For whenever Mass is said, we re-enact the Passion and Death of Our Lord; and on this Christmas Day we do this in celebration of His Birth. . . . At this same time of all the year that we celebrate at once the Birth of Our Lord and His Passion and Death upon the Cross. . . . It is only in these our Christian mysteries that we can rejoice and mourn at once for the same reason.

The Savior who was crucified and the Lord who was raised was at some time (unknown to us) and in some manner (symbolically represented) born into the world of men. Apart from the cross and resurrection, such a birth would obviously have no significance. The manner of Jesus' conception is a deduction from the sequel, not the origin and ground of our faith in Christ as Lord. Whatever we may make of the virgin birth, it affirms the acceptance of the initiative of God in man's redemption. The details of the Nativity story (strictly, stories) are homiletically valuable symbols of the condescension of the Son of God, a voluntary subjection to humility more graphically and historically presented in the cross (cf. Phil. 2:6-11).

The greatest service the Christian church could receive from its preachers would be the proclamation of the faith that God had entered into the involvements of human life and triumphed for all men in and through them. The recovery of this message, its appropriation by the individual and its application in the church and society, would restore the joy of Christmas in the Christian sense of the word "joy" and substitute it for its counterfeit, concocted by the self-stimulation of the world.

The Epiphany. Here the chronological problem becomes acute and can best be solved by abandoning it in favor of emphasis upon the meaning of Christ's presence in human history. The visit of the Magi as "event" is clearly symbolical. It affords by this fact a good time to discuss the combined historical and symbolical nature of the Christian message and would helpfully compel the preacher to deal with the apologetic problem. The theme can best be described as *God's availability to all mankind*. This holds also if some of the other traditional Epiphany themes of Scripture are emphasized along with or in preference to the Wise Men — Jesus' baptism, the transfiguration, the turning of water into wine, etc., from the Fourth Gospel, and their counterparts from the Old Testament, Jacob at Bethel, the burning bush, Elijah on Horeb, etc.

The emphasis of this season would be the universality of Christianity rather than its particularity, but arising from the " offense " of its particularity, as it does on either side from the birth and death of Jesus. The avoidance of themes like the baptism came from the fears of heresy involved in adoptionist tendencies in a period of theological controversy. At some periods the emphasis of the season has fallen upon the humanity of Jesus rather than upon his manifestation of the divine power, creating some confusion with the traditional theme of Lent. The suggestion made here is an extended discussion of the revelatory significance of Christ's impact upon the world and the timeless and universal quality of that impact.

McArthur suggests, rather, a treatment of the ministry of Jesus from now until Lent to be completed in Lent on the basis of the " watershed " theory of the Synoptics — that there is a distinct " frontier " at the point of the transfiguration but with no " absolute contrast between the ministry and the Passion . . ." (*The Christian Year*, pp. 78–80). This has its own liturgical as well as exegetical difficulties, and in the modern world a season in which the preacher is compelled to deal with the claims of Christianity to be a universal religion and the hope of cosmic redemption would be a constructive element in a fully rounded presentation. The " missionary " element involved is extremely important over against a militant communism and an equally militant eclecticism.

Pre-Lent. The tendency in liturgical history to lengthen the discipline preparatory to Easter has done as much as anything to cause havoc to any reasonable scheme and has left us with three Sundays preparatory to a season of preparation. They have been the despair of liturgiologists, pastors, preachers, and even sacristans. The themes inherited from the medieval missals (and reflected in *The Book of Common Prayer* as in the Lectionary appended to *The Book of Common Worship*) are difficult to co-ordinate. They may be taken, however, to suggest a preliminary review of the personal life of the Christian and so to afford an application of the Epiphany theme to the individual in preparation for the self-discipline of Lent. So Septuagesima suggests the Christian warrior or athlete and his individual rewards; the second Sunday (Sexagesima), the tribulations of the Christian and his victory within and over them; the third Sunday (Quinquagesima), the all-important personal appropriation of *agapē* and the call to follow in this "way." This suggests the need for individual self-examination and also prepares for the recalling at the end of Lent that to be a Christian is to follow Christ in the way of the cross.

Lent. The pre-Lenten Sundays may, of course, be taken up into either Epiphany (McArthur) or Lent. The decision might be left open so that an early Easter would not unnecessarily curtail Epiphany nor a late one unduly prolong it. Lent, ending as it does with the Passion and beginning traditionally with the "temptations," affords an obvious opportunity to deal with "the ministry of the Son of Man." This is a salutary requirement in a period when doubts have arisen about the actuality of Jesus' life or of our ability to know anything about it. The theme can find a good basis in a treatment of the Synoptic Gospels, of Mark in particular with its dynamic Christian framework (just as the Fourth Gospel is appropriate for Epiphany).

Since the cross is the central fact and symbol of the faith, and atonement is its central meaning, and since the day on which it is observed is a weekday, it is well to plan the treatment so that a more concentrated consideration of the Passion becomes the main theme of the last two Sundays before Easter. The theme of Lent may obviously have widely varied modes of presentation, but in general it can be stated as *the human work of Christ*. This may come to a head in the fifth Sunday (known for long as " Passion Sunday ") with the " Passion Predictions " and " Behold, we go up to Jerusalem " as fitting gospel themes, and in Holy Week with its consideration of the Last Week as arranged by the Synoptic Evangelists (possibly originally for this very liturgical purpose).

Here it may be well to note that the minister must pay heed to the current and local customs of the people. In my experience churches have been thronged on Palm Sunday, attracted by the charming but incidental pageantry associated with the popular title. There is no need to abandon this, but it should be made incidental to the reading of the Passion and the preaching of the cross. Many more people are available on this Sunday than there will be on Friday (for hardly anywhere is Good Friday a " holiday "), and a rare opportunity to present the heart of the gospel can be lost by preoccupation with the triumphal entry. Perhaps in this way we would also escape the canard that the very people who cried " Hosanna " on Sunday cried " Crucify him " on Friday, an ingrained cliché that has but poor basis in any real historical study of the Gospels. Any devotions offered on Good Friday or the other days of Holy Week are likely to be attended by "the faithful" and represent a very different problem from the ordinary public service.

Easter. The churches, even the liturgical churches, have, by and large, lost by default any real celebration of the forty-day celebration of the greatest Christian day of all. The great forty (or even fifty) days after Easter traditionally were intended to balance the forty days of Lent. Easter in the ordinary church presents the greatest challenge and the most frustrating opportunity of the year. Again the problems of myth and history stare the preacher in the face and cannot be shirked. Yet he is in a better position than at Christmas. Physically the worshipers (if the majority may be called such) are more widely awake. They are there largely from the impetus of persisting social custom compounded of inertia, spring fever, sartorial display, and a lingering superstitious hope that they may learn of their own indubitable immortality. Can the church compete with the birds and blossoms in any message of hope? The theme, however, is not personal immortality any more than it is racial immortality or the annual renewal of nature. The theme is the resurrection of Christ as the first fruits of those who believe and the inauguration of a new creation. The solid rock is the faith of the first Christians as expressed in the New Testament, the faith that in sober historical fact provided the foundation of the Christian church. This is the fact to be proclaimed and explained, and the New Testament has but one explanation that, however we may state it, has marked every page.

There are people present at Easter whom the preacher will not address again from the pulpit until next Easter —

unless something is done now to excite their interest in coming again to hear and experience more. The true worshipers among whom they have seated themselves will get much of what they need from the service and the preaching need not be primarily concerned with them. Yet the sermon cannot be pure *apologia*. It must be an affirmative proclamation made in such manner that people may know the preacher is honestly aware of their difficulties and prepared in time to deal with them. The renewal of the resurrection faith of the first Christians is the result to be hoped for. This is the objective rather than a catering to the personal and selfish hope that people who pay no attention to the gospel will somehow survive the death of their bodies.

The Sundays between Easter and Ascension allow for a fuller development of the theme of Easter along the rich New Testament lines, involving the renewal of man, of society, and of nature itself. Equally important, these Sundays provide an opportunity to deal with the ascension, which, traditionally marked on the fortieth day and hence necessarily a weekday, is the most neglected occasion and theme of all.

Ascension. In the New Testament, apart from The Acts of the Apostles (as distinct from the Gospel of Luke), the resurrection and the ascension are so closely involved as to be virtually indistinguishable. There has been a tendency liturgically to confine the ascension to that absence of our Lord which involved the coming of the Holy Spirit. This is usefully Johannine but does not exhaust the meaning of the occasion. The resurrection involves a restoration or exaltation to " the right hand of God."

Here there is a double meaning. First, Christ is King; from the degradation of death on the cross he has been lifted up to be the ultimate authority and source of power for man and arbiter of human destiny. When the creed says, "from thence he shall come to judge," we are given the answer to the consideration of the destiny of man mentioned above in connection with Advent. Secondly, by his exaltation Christ has become intercessor and *sole* mediator between God and man. This aspect of the ascension is sorely neglected, and yet it is essential to a proper understanding of Christian prayer and worship. Its neglect is the fruitful cause of the exaltation of Mary and the saints to the place that belongs to Christ alone. It is by virtue of human experience that the Christ who is LORD is also equipped to be mediator and that prayer "in his name" carries the assurance that human needs are understood at first hand in heaven.

This is to put the matter somewhat crudely, but it needs to be stated bluntly if a predominant theme of the New Testament is not to be lost sight of. No aspect of the cruci-fixion-resurrection-ascension complex, which is the heart of the gospel, can more readily be presented to meet effec-tively the predicament of men as it is now commonly under-stood under such terms as "estrangement" and "aliena-tion" and other aspects of a "broken relationship." The Sundays after Easter, treating the ascension not as a climax of Easter nor as a prelude to Pentecost, but as an immedi-ate implication of the resurrection, could be one of the most fruitful periods of the year for the preacher. If used intelligently and, one might add, passionately, this could be the most ready means of overcoming the virtual loss of attention that plagues the churches from Easter on.

Whitsunday. It can be said that the ascension testifies to the extension of Christ's work in heaven and the activity of the Holy Spirit to its extension on earth. What better way could there be to state the value of the festival of Pentecost? Degraded to a celebration of the birthday of the church, it loses its major significance. The doctrine of the Holy Spirit is not so much neglected theologically as it is impossible to distinguish it in clear logical terms from the doctrine of Christ and the church. There is a valid reason for this. It is the primary function of the Holy Spirit to testify to Christ and not to himself.

The relationship of the Holy Spirit to prayer and to the church in all its aspects provides a continuing matter for exposition through the rest of the year. For this reason as well as for others there have always been those (including McArthur recently) who have commended the practice of the Roman Catholic Church in naming the remaining Sundays of the church year " Sundays After Pentecost " instead of the more recently introduced title, " Sundays After Trinity." The life of the Christian and the work of the church is inconceivable without the Holy Spirit. Yet there is something to be said on the other side, and in England the octave of Whitsunday became the feast of Trinity.

Trinity. Trinity Sunday looks forward in that it is the beginning of a distinct segment of the ecclesiastical year. It is true that unlike the other great festivals, it commemorates no event in the history of redemption. As the mark of a doctrine, it has, however, the value of summing up all that has gone before. As was said above, it is hardly possible to define closely the doctrine of the Holy Spirit. Any attempt to do so involves a discussion of the Trinity in Unity. As the beginning of a whole " half " of the preaching year, Trinity Sunday has a value. It reminds us that as a matter of fact Christianity is not a, so to speak, " pneumatic " faith but a Trinitarian one. The development and outgrowth of the gospel revelation is not a Spirit-faith but a faith in God the Father, Son, and Holy Ghost.

This suggests a second aspect. The first part of the Christian year has been aptly called dominical, not because it follows the life of Christ, but because it deals with the revelation of God in Christ. The second half of the year has no all-embracing title and so appears " empty." From the point of view of the preaching of the gospel in its fullness, however, this evaluation would miss the essential nature of the Christian faith as existential, concerned not with dogma alone but with a divinely oriented living of life.

The " openness " of the Trinity season also provides that element of freedom, the absence of which the opponents of an ordered scheme most often urge against it. After the salient points of revelation have been rehearsed, it is necessary to ask what is their application to the life of man and the work of the church at large. The Sundays after Trinity might well be thought of as the practical half or the application of the faith. If the attention of the church were confined annually and exclusively to the great creedal moments, there would indeed be a failure to perceive the full significance of any one of them or of the whole. The areas of life called ecclesiastical, political, economical, sociological, and the like would remain, as it were, unbaptized. Yet the Christian church is not interested in these topics as separated disciplines or as manifestations of a " pneumatic " life, but is compelled to ask, What is a Trinitarian understanding of the church and its life, of society, of politics, of economic and international affairs? These urgent matters must be brought into relation to the faith in a Father who creates and sends his Son who redeems and from whom proceeds the Holy Spirit who sanctifies the created and redeemed — and these, not simply as individuals, but as members of a church, of a society, of an era, and of the human race.

In this section of the ecclesiastical year is all the freedom to deal with topics of vital importance and the obligation to apply the faith to the daily preoccupations of men. This is not to say that this will not be done in the dominical half. Rather, it is necessary to show that the preaching of the creedal moments is unrealistic and fruitless unless held in close connection with immedate concerns. Apart from this, incarnation and atonement have no very real meaning. The difference, briefly phrased, is that in the dominical series the center of attention is the revelation; in the " free " Sundays the center of attention is the relationship of religion to practical matters; in neither can each interest be present to the exclusion of the other or Christianity loses its essential validity. To attempt thus to put the matter in words brings us to the need to discuss method, and to this we must turn after the summary of the discussion of the nature of an annual scheme.

Any scheme of annual observances intended to provide a basis to preaching the gospel in its fullness may be summarized in its essentials in this way. The center and pivot must be the solemn observance of the crucifixion and resurrection as divine acts, in history, of atonement and redemption. It is fitting that this be preceded by a period of personal and corporate preparation to appropriate the salvation offered and that it be followed by a period in which the broader aims of the redemption of a people for God and of the whole cosmos receive attention. Within this plan there should be an extension at one end for the consideration of the gospel story, including the work of Jesus, his ministry on earth, and, at the other end, an extension for consideration of his continuing work in heaven as mediator and on earth through the Holy Spirit. It is appropriate that the plan begin with attention to God's invasion of history culminating in the incarnation, and that it close with a summation of the faith in the triune God that the dominical half of the year has rehearsed. The provision of an ample period unmarked by seasonal or special celebrations is necessary for the working out of this faith in the individual life of the Christian and the corporate life of the church. Its application to the world at large would fittingly come to a climax as the round begins again with a reminder of the ultimate denouement when Christ will present the Kingdom to his Father and God will be all in all.

So to express the general course, working backward and forward from Holy Week and Easter is at one and the same time to indicate the value of the traditional scheme and to suggest points at which it needs to be freed from bondage to a chronological conception and too great a dependence on outmoded literal adherence to the Scriptures. The task of revisers of lectionaries that are to provide a basis for preaching and teaching and for the pastoral work of building up the people of God is to recover the essential kerygma and *paradosis* of the New Testament and to arrange it in cyclical form in periods rather than in days and to co-ordinate with it Old Testament material that will disclose the preparation in " sacred history" for the revelation in Christ.

It would be entirely in the realm of phantasy for revisers to ignore the traditional ecclesiastical year, but a thorough study of its development (like that of McArthur) discloses the basic points as distinct from the haphazard growth of subsidiary occasions and material. The incoherent state of some of the lections (especially eucharistic)

of the traditional liturgical churches reveals a distortion of
originally coherent and integrated plans by adaptation to
local conditions and temporary fashions. The original
plans, even where they can be recovered, are not necessarily the best guide to our present needs. We have to take
account of developments in Biblical studies and the situation in which the churches find themselves in the modern
world. Yet caution needs to be exercised in order that one
value is not unduly disregarded — namely, the still exist-
ing unity extending over large areas that makes traditional
the reading of certain portions of the Bible on specific occasions. This would in part be taken care of by the " fixed
points " that have their classical Scriptural expression.

On the other hand, the modern view of the Bible has
sometimes caused lectionary revisers to exclude all readings that do not fit into a scheme of " *Religionsgeschichte* "
or progressive revelation through records that can be more
or less verified. This has the effect of ignoring the work of
the Biblical compilers who selected and placed in juxta-
position certain passages and of making incomprehensible
many of the typological features of the New Testament. It
is for the preacher to deal with this element as he has
been trained to do rather than for him to be delivered from
the need to do so by never being confronted with it. His
presentation would only thereby be impoverished. This,
however, brings us back to the question of the value of an
ordered scheme for the preacher, and his purpose and
method in using it.

IV

PREACHER, BIBLE, AND PEOPLE

THE APOSTLE PAUL, in Gal. 1:1-14, makes the forthright declaration, "If I sought the favor of men, I should no longer be a servant of Christ." This is the same Paul who claims in Romans to have been called to the apostleship to the Gentiles and to have received through Christ grace to carry out his particular mission (Rom. 1:1). Of any preacher we must assume that beyond the authority conferred by ordination in his own particular communion he is aware of having been laid under a higher claim. He is set aside for a distinct function that is defined by that call and not by the response he can elicit by his own skill nor by the welcome the people accord him. The ubiquity of commercialized entertainment creates the danger that minister and people will lose sight of this higher motivation by adopting the judgments exercised in that secular realm. Sponsors of radio and television seek for programs and performances that will be welcomed by their listeners or viewers. They aim ultimately to effect changes in the buying habits of the audience by adapting themselves to the current entertainment predilections of the people.

This is precisely what Paul says he cannot do — and still be a servant of Jesus Christ. He cannot combine entertainment and salesmanship (an accurate but unfortunate description of some popular preaching). Paul says specifically that he is not a " huckster " or " peddler " of God's Word (see the Greek of II Cor. 2:17, or RSV). As a " steward of the mysteries," he must be faithful to the Christ whose servant he is and to the mystery of which he is also necessarily a servant. In the very necessities of the case a judgment is involved (I Cor. 4:1-4). We can judge nothing, not even our own ministry, from a human point of view (II Cor. 5:16-17). He is an " ambassador " (v. 20), and an ambassador does not create foreign policy; he interprets a given policy to aliens and applies it to those affairs in which there is a common interest between his own government and that of the nation to which he is accredited. (F. D. Coggan has given a good account of Pauline terminology in his book, *The Ministry of the Word.*) To be a steward of " mysteries " means that the message, correctly described as a mystery, must be disclosed *to* the preacher as well as *by* the preacher to the hearers. Here is one of the fundamental justifications for placing the preacher under the authority of some scheme of Biblical material as a basis for his ministry of the Word.

The day has gone when rhetorical devices sufficed to carry the message. (The preacher no less than the politician has taken a long time to learn the lesson that Lincoln taught.) The political forum in democratic countries has now almost entirely foresworn the rhetorical. The demand of a literate public (especially of its younger elements) is for a reasonable, coherent, convincing subject matter, expressed in contemporary language, adequately illuminated, reinforced by the sincerity of the speaker. Rhetoric is nowhere more suspect than in matters that are proper to the pulpit. The authority the sermon carries, therefore, will depend upon a sense that the preacher is "under orders," concerned, himself, to discover and to apply the truth and meaning of the gospel that he seeks to commend.

It soon becomes apparent when a preacher confines himself to certain passages of Scripture or to themes familiar to himself and in which he is at home — so much at home that the impression of mechanical ease is hard to escape. Much of modern preaching, even in liturgical churches, has been on subjects that have no necessary connection with each other beyond the preacher's interest in them and no necessary relation to the gospel except as he conceives it. This may make for a certain liveliness of presentation and carry with it a feeling of sincerity in the modern sense. With reference to the field of entertainment, David Riesman puts it this way: " It means that the source of criteria for judgment has shifted from the content of the performance and its goodness or badness, aesthetically speaking, to the personality of the performer. He is judged for his attitude toward the audience, an attitude which is either sincere or insincere, rather than by his relation to his craft, that is, his honesty and skill." This hardly fulfills the expectation of the Christian church that the preacher will present not his own interests, but God's; not his own gospel, but Christ's. Paul transgressed the bounds of polite language when describing such a partisan performance (Gal. 5:12, in the Greek). His prime concern, as he expressed it, was to " placard," or display, Christ crucified (Gal. 3:1).

People and minister alike are delivered from this snare of the " topic " if the preacher, with due submission and intelligent freedom, pays attention to the exposition of a fully rounded cycle of Scripture that he has not himself chosen. It places him under the obligation to discover the meaning of passages that do not immediately appeal to

him as congenial to his own interests or specialized training and to discover why the church has in the past (or by
recent decision) found this selection important. It is often
by means of the very necessity to break through his own
inertia or ignorance that he arrives at the discovery of a
new facet of truth that will enable him to come before his
people with something of the enthusiasm of a discoverer.
Such enthusiasm is a valuable and potent substitute for
applied rhetoric.

A still more effective process takes place when, in a
cyclical plan, a passage that seems to have been exhausted
in its first treatment is explored again for further meaning
and relevance to a situation that is not the same as before.
It is usual for the first encounter to satisfy itself with an
over-all treatment. Subsequent encounters, if seriously un-
dertaken, lead to deeper analysis and concentration upon
aspects inadequately developed in the summary treatment.
This is an invaluable homiletical training because the beginning preacher usually suffers from saying too little
about too much and needs, above all, to learn to say a lot
more about a great deal less. By this process he learns to
overcome the tendency to accumulate assertions that are
passed over without examination, illustration, or application. Instead, he is forced to analyze, look for similes and
analogies, and reveal the area and mode of application.
Too often a minister changes churches within a few years
and merely repeats what he said in his previous pulpit. Or
he seeks new topics rather than the treatment in depth
and detail of the old.

C. S. Lewis, in his *A Preface to Paradise Lost*, has shown
that repetition is an important factor in oral poetry of the
epic type where, for instance, " stock phrases " bring a
sense of reassurance and achievement to the listeners. The

same observation might be made about the cyclical re-appearance of Biblical themes. Far from being bored with repetition, the regularly attending congregation finds the renewal of attention to passages in process of becoming familiar a welcome reassurance and a cumulative means of illumination. The connection of some of these passages with certain seasons of the Christian year has the further value of recall. The worshiper, more often than the preacher supposes, becomes conscious not only of his failures in appropriating the message but also of his real growth in reception of grace. To speak personally, as one who has from birth belonged to the same communion (though to different branches), the greatest sense of growth and continuity has come from annually repeated encounters with the same Scriptural lections, inviting and compelling deeper consideration independent of the preacher but greatly helped when he has dealt directly and honestly with the material provided. This goes back to long before I had any idea of entering the ministry. When I came into a new situation in an entirely new place, the reassurance of familiar material had two effects. It held me secure in the sense that the church is one and the people of God universal. The fresh and excitingly relevant treatment then provided by the preacher I was fortunate enough to find (Dr. Beverley D. Tucker) was a large element in persuading me that I was called to try to do the same for my own generation.

Here, then, is suggested a basis for that authority which is not imposed from above by dictation but consists in a three-way connection and interaction between a church, a minister, and a congregation. *The church* provides the plan — whether derived from tradition or newly constructed by representative means and subject to revision on the basis of use. It expects that the preacher will use it intelligently with reasonable (not fantatical) diligence and in preference to his uncontrolled whims. *The preacher* uses the plan to provide him with some guidance to the mind of the church and meets it as a demand for some discipline of his own concern in the interests of the church as a whole. It enables him to fulfill his obligation to speak for the church and relieves him of the need to make his own ideas convincing. His contribution is his own experience of Christ, his knowledge of the whole range of Scripture and of the Christian interpretation of it, and his sense of the points of need among his particular people in his own peculiar times. *The people* contribute chiefly regularity of attendance, but they also share in the process by affording their pastor some sense of the problem of acceptance, of the areas where application of the gospel is necessary, and of the difficulties inherent in responding to it. They become aware that they are not dealing with a man who happens to have some good ideas that he expresses felicitously, but with an agent of an ancient and tried faith, which he serves with humility, and with the servant of One to whom he seeks to introduce them.

Adherence to a plan not exclusively the preacher's own takes the people beyond the preacher. This is sorely needed. (What is said here and elsewhere about the preacher's use of lections in the pulpit applies also to the function of the readings in the service of worship and can be assumed where applicable.) Too often people are attached to a minister rather than to the Christian faith or even to a church. They come and go, ally or disassociate themselves, according as they like the ideas the minister has. The skill and personality of the minister can never (and should not) be eliminated, but he defeats the purpose he professes when the presentation he offers leads to himself and not to Christ. As John Oman (I believe) has said, no minister can at the same time exalt both himself and Christ. The demands that regular adherence to a scheme of basic material supplies do a good deal to prevent this barrier from arising because they induce in the preacher a healthy sense of humility before the Word of God.

The factor of regular attendance deserves further notice. Disregarding the small minority who attend from the inertia of habit, parental authority, or some other compulsive factor, regular attendance must be secured as a rule by two channels and one means. First, there is the witness of those who do attend. Others, hearing and observing them, wish to discover the source of the help they have received. Then there are those who happen to come, seeking or " shopping around," or by that unexplained prompting that the Christian recognizes as the work of the Holy Spirit. In either case, a great deal depends upon the service and sermon that the newcomer encounters. Here the sermon may succeed in spite of the service or the service in spite of the sermon. Ideally, as said above, the two should be so integrated as mutually to reinforce each other.

The great problem, with the newcomer in view, is so to preach on every occasion that the gospel, in some essential aspect, is proclaimed without every sermon being either a summary of the faith or a reiteration of some such theme as justification by faith. This is not so impossible as it sounds. It may be crudely indicated by saying that it is not necessary to tear down the wall of a room to find out what the room is like inside. It is sufficient to open a door or to look through a window. In fact, a great deal can be seen and a real impression formed by looking through the keyhole — enough to know whether one does or does not want to see more. So with preaching. The whole range of creedal or kerygmatic affirmation does not need to be rehearsed. A preacher deeply committed to the gospel needs only to deal with one aspect of it, provided it *is* an aspect of it, and to deal with it honestly and relevantly. The newcomer will know, if his intention is serious, that he has caught a glimpse of something new (or been recalled to something forgotten or discarded), that he has been promised further and fuller revelation, and that what he has seen does concern his situation in the world in which he lives.

Before we pass on to consider how this may be done, it is necessary to observe that the plan of material basic to the worship and preaching must be designed for this purpose — capable of serving its purpose as a moment in a larger cycle but also affording a real contact with the essential message as a whole. The church we visualize and the preaching we intend to discuss is not the street-corner type of hit-and-run evangelism (which has a technique of its own), nor the " one-night-stand " effort of the " visiting preacher." This last probably should be abandoned on all occasions except those which call for the presence of a specialist or a preacher having some significance for the occasion as, for instance, an ordination, dedication of a building, inauguration of a special program. The sole function of the preacher in a local church is the building up of the people of God. This embraces basically three things: the securing of new converts and their attachment to the corporate life, the nurture of the congregation in its Christian experience, and the imparting of a real sense of the church universal and active participation in its mission to all mankind.

In the service of any of these facets of the task, the relevance of the sermon is essential if it is to carry the authority we have been looking for and of which the provision of a plan and its consistent use by the minister are only the basis. There has to be communication with the actual people present in their real situation. This was true long before existentialism came into vogue — as far back as when Paul said, " I have become all things to all men, that I might by all means save some " (I Cor. 9:22). Farther back, Paul's ancestors, the prophets, spoke of God's interest in the Syrians, Assyrians, and Cyrus. The preacher today is no longer addressing eighth-century Israel, or first-century Hellenists, or twelfth-century lords and serfs, or eighteenth-century squires. He is addressing people who live in the atomic age under the conditions we tried to describe in the first chapter. More accurately and seriously, he is trying to interpret what " saith the Lord " to this day. (This phrase is usually associated with prophecy rather than with preaching. R. B. Y. Scott has produced a careful examination of the distinction and how far it may be applied in his article in the first issue of the *Canadian Journal of Theology,* " Is Preaching Prophecy? ")

No change of period changes the gospel, and this should be self-evident. But unless the present time is taken account of, the gospel is not heard — in any effective sense of the word " heard." To be able to hear, people have to be made *ready to hear*. Any parson who has had a pastoral ministry knows the person who suddenly exclaims, " I never knew (or heard) that before," although he or she has probably been exposed to it often. I remember a woman who said to me, " That is the best news I ever heard," but the news was that Christ died for us while we were still sinners and this she had often been told but had not until then been prepared to hear.

It is too much to ask people to transport themselves bodily to Biblical times. If the gospel is a saving power, still it must be capable of demonstration that it is gospel to the people we are. Yet I have heard sermon after sermon that might as easily have been preached (often to better advantage) in the 1300's or the 1600's as in the 1900's. This is a wonderful demonstration of the continuity of the theme treated, but it is also purely academic and requires no involvement on the part of the hearer. It is all too easy for the preacher to present the fruits of his own secluded study, a report from the library so to speak, unaware of the actual people before him.

R. H. Fuller, in *What Is Liturgical Preaching?* says, " Indeed, we might almost say that we live in an age which is marked by a cult of the relevant " (p. 16). He argues that preoccupation with what is immediately and directly relevant is dangerous. " For the gospel is concerned with man's *ultimate* needs, with his need for forgiveness and redemption. Men and women are usually conscious of their less-than-ultimate needs, their need for security, for deliverance from anxiety and frustration, for the attainment of social acceptance and the like " (p. 16, Fuller's italics). The gospel, Fuller truly says, must not be trimmed down to the measure of people's needs. It may first expose their needs " as trivial and false " and reveal to them their ultimate need. Dr. Fuller writes from the point of view of England, though not without immediate experience of American life. There is very probably a more concerned and even exaggerated effort to deal with the manifestations of people's immediate needs in the American pulpit than elsewhere. The charge of " activism " is widely made and can be justified. The title of Dr. Reuel Howe's book,

Man's Need and God's Action, is itself a reminder that the gospel is relevant and designed to be so. The method suggested by the title is perhaps not sound as a basis for theology, since it is a truism that God's love and mercy are not conditioned, not even by man's needs. This can be demonstrated from Jesus' own practice and teaching (see, e.g., my book *The Jesus of the Parables*).

But to hold that the gospel is a response to man's need is not necessarily to affirm that the response is *produced by the need.* On the other hand, the mighty acts of God, which rest solely on his own initiative, must come to man as felt response to known needs. Dr. Howe has convincingly shown that personal deprivations may make the appropriation of the gospel message impossible until some break-through is made. Parish and clinical experience alike testify that the approach to the ultimate problem and the meeting of the ultimate need can usually be effected only *by dealing with the immediate need.* It is the task of the preacher to proclaim the unconditioned love of God manifest climactically in the cross and, in so doing, to break through the awareness of surface problems to reveal to the people the actual danger in which they stand. Yet the unconditioned love of God must be so proclaimed as evidently to answer the predicament in which man finds himself — as indeed it does and is intended to do.

This can be done because much of the Biblical material deals with the ordinary felt needs of people on a level that sometimes seems naïve, hardly to be compared at first sight with the analysis modern psychology offers. Thus, in John's Gospel, the need of more wine for a marriage produces a story that, on its deeper levels, deals actually with the relation of the law to the gospel (John 2:1-11). Mark can tell the story of a man's need for sight in such manner and context that it becomes a story of the vision of the Christ who must be followed "on the way" (Mark 10:46-52). Not to mention the down-to-earth stories of the Old Testament, the parables of Jesus deal with seeming trivialities and yet raise the issue of the Kingdom of God in all its ramifications. The analysis open to modern ministers who have received a basic clinical training provides a deeper understanding of the way in which the gospel reaches below the surface. The composite story of the paralytic to whom Jesus said, "Son, thy sins be forgiven thee," penetrates the reality of the power of sin to incapacitate even the physical response of the will (Mark 2:1-12). There is awaiting discovery a relevance in the Biblical material that is not always apparent on the surface.

When, therefore, Dr. Fuller says, "Our starting point must be, not the people's needs but the gospel in its fullness" (p. 17), one must agree in essence but raise a question as to the place of the assertion on the level of practice and method. The provision of a basic plan and loyal adherence to it for which we have argued provides the starting point of the full gospel. The preacher must always be aware of that " given " factor with which he deals and the Lord whom, through it, he serves. He cannot be a man-pleaser. Yet he is commissioned to serve the people and them he must know. How is he to get beneath their constant and immediate preoccupation, how detach them from the ethos of a secularized time, how convince them that the gospel is not remote, outmoded, academic? How, especially, is he to reach young people who lack even the rudiments of a religious nurture, to whom the very words and atmosphere of the church are utterly alien, and persuade them that their fears, their frenzied clutching after security, and their paralyzing self-consciousness are matters with which the gospel deals and for which it offers an answer?

Certainly there is no value in " the revelant " unless it is at the same time the very truth of God, and the preacher may preach nothing less than Him who is the Truth. Our argument is that a plan based on the Scriptures in the context of the church protects him from neglecting the heart of the gospel in favor of interesting topics. Yet I recall my theological professor's insistence that two people are always involved in the transmission of the truth — the teller, who intends the truth by what he speaks, and the listener, who is to receive and understand it as the truth intended. It is an essential part of the truth to proclaim that *Christ died for sinners,* but each of those four words in its context needs to be elucidated and " brought near " if the four together are to make to modern man the sense they intend. Contemporary man does not know (and even thinks he does not care) about Messiahship. His ideas of sin are either remote or wrong (i.e., moralistic). The whole notion of atonement in both of these connections is either totally obscure or else repugnant. There is no way in actual practice to start with the gospel except by rehearsing the story. Even so, the whole point is whether the story is still relevant or merely an ancient myth.

It may be, as C. S. Lewis suggested in *The Screwtape Letters,* the work of the devil that prompts people to ask every question except Is it true? but it is urgently with this ubiquitous work of evil that the preacher has to contend. " Proof " has little importance to the modern man. Truth today will be of vital concern to the individual only as its acceptance as true makes a difference in his actual situation. Here is where the work has to be done. One can go beyond what Lewis has said and observe that a further element in the preacher's problem is this: There is a demand for "truth," but what is meant popularly by the question, Is it true? is the junior-aged child's query, Did it actually happen just so? Even if that could be answered, there would be the further question, If so, what of it? In the confines of the theologian's study it may be possible to say it does not matter, for instance, whether we know anything factual about Jesus. To say this, however, to the modern man is to refuse to answer his question and to invite him to dismiss the whole matter. Perhaps in this he has a sounder instinct than has the scholar. Before we can meet the test of truth, we have to deal with the sense in which the word "truth" is used. It is of the essence of the Biblical faith that whatever else may be meant by truth, it must include some assurance that a historical revelation actually happened. Radically to demythologize the gospel presupposes actually a serious attempt to re-mythologize it, and this involves nothing less than the presentation of fact in a form relevant to the thought modes and active interests of the people with whom we deal — at least in such manner as to take the first step toward changing those interests and modes of thought.

We need, then, to go on to heed the words of David Roberts in his book of sermons, *The Grandeur and Misery of Man*. Roberts was a preacher who himself knew both the gospel and modern man and the tension in which they stood toward each other. He says, "*Let us start, then, with man*, no matter how much such a proposal may horrify some theologians" (p. 61, italics added). Before making this statement, he has prepared the way for it by saying: "Sometimes, we *have* been guilty of talking about the existence of God in such a way that it has no discernible bearing upon the decisive events of human life. Whenever God becomes simply an idea that we want to defend against competing ideas, then it is quite right to say that we have lost touch with the real issue." So, " Let us start with man. . . . Let us start with his hopes and fears, his assets and liabilities, his power and weakness. Let us start with his inner battle between slavery and freedom. In that instant the problem is not how we can bring God into connection with our theme, but how we can possibly avoid him" (p. 61). The aim of the preacher could hardly be better stated or his best method more succinctly characterized — to show people that the human situation compels attention to the gospel.

This is also a profound statement of the apologetic task mentioned above as a preoccupying demand upon the preacher. For the minister in his contacts with people, apologetics does not initially concern the justification of this or that Christian philosophy, theological tenet, or moral counsel against competing theories, but concerns *the relevance of the matter as a whole.* R. E. C. Browne feels that it lies at the level of basic meaning. " The question for many modern people, Christian and non-Christian, is not about moral behavior but about meaningful behavior. Are human speech and action significant? " (*The Ministry of the Word,* p. 98). It may be put fundamentally in the form of the question, So what? That is to say, " Even supposing God exists at all and that he is revealed in the life and death and resurrection of Christ, what of it? " It is heart-rending to sit in church, especially in a church that has obviously provided in its service a basic plan for the presentation of the gospel, and hear the preacher introduce his sermon with a discussion of the background of the Biblical lection or of the liturgical occasion or any one of the many matters that immediately discloses the *preacher's* interest rather than any sense of the urgent needs or problems of the people. These matters may be presented, and presented effectively, but their introduction is calculated to dissipate attention on the part of those who most need the message until it has been explained why the liturgical occasion is worth noting or in what way a knowledge of the Biblical background illuminates the modern scene.

The problem, then, of liturgical preaching, in the sense of the use of an ordered scheme of using the Bible in worship and preaching, is the discovery of the point of contact. This takes careful preliminary work. Without serious preparation the preacher is defeated before he begins. The preparation must be of himself as well as of his message. This is a truism, but it applies forcefully in the limited area we are discussing, because unless the minister daily muses upon the Scriptures, meditates upon the overall plan he is to use, and applies it to his own life, he is little likely to be even interested in its application to anyone else — unless he is a hypocrite in the root sense of the word. The sermon must start with people, but the preparation to do so starts in the study (assuming prayer to begin with).

This will involve, first of all, a consideration of the material offered by the church to be presented in worship and sermon on the occasion concerned. There may be a choice available (some lectionary schemes have this provision). Such choice may already have been made in the decision to follow one set of lections this year and another the next. If there is no immediate indication that one passage rather than another is decidedly relevant, the choice should be deferred until some preliminary study has been done. Relevance and "usability" (if I may use the word) often are disclosed below the surface. The first suggestion that comes to mind may be exactly the one to be avoided as reflecting nothing but the interest or pet theme of the preacher. At this point the tools provided in commentaries and books, better still by a retranslation from the original (or the reading of several versions), are valuable. A little digging may throw a quite new light upon the passage. A recalling of the personality of the Biblical author, or of the time and occasion of writing, the identity of the original readers, the circumstances and interests of the time and the message of the book as a whole — all of this may at some point suggest the means of interest and contact. What is needed is an analysis of the Biblical passage such as will reveal the human predicament with which it deals and the answer the Biblical revelation makes to it. This may be more like a meditation than an investigation, and those who are familiar with the Ignatian method will have a good clue to my intention. (The steps taken are vital to the process, but extremely rarely should they reappear in the sermon itself.)

After we have arrived at the point where human interest and Biblical revelation meet, the sermon itself can begin. What is the human situation? How can it be presented in a manner to enable the people to see it is *their* situation or that it is symptomatic of their real and more ultimate problem? Hence the sermon itself may begin with an analysis (or picture that serves the same purpose) of the human predicament. This will lead to the point that there is no human answer, though this need not be stated in so many words. This is the place at which to introduce the Biblical material — but not the step-by-step analysis of it. The preacher's work on it in the study has prepared him to reveal the fact that it deals in essence with exactly this situation.

Its application now raises the matter to a new level where one of three things may happen: understanding may be gained, an answer may be suggested, or the relevance of God's acts may be made clear. The " application " in the homiletical sense virtually makes itself. Was it not Spurgeon who said that the sermon begins where its applicability begins? To follow this method means that the sermon begins at the beginning, for there the matter to which it is to be applied is at once suggested. Furthermore, such a beginning provides unity in the sermon, for the end will be practically a restatement on a Christian level of the matter first introduced. By this means also the preacher is delivered from the need to create an artificial means of gaining interest at the start. He starts with the interests of the people, and there is no need to explain to them why he is going to speak about the matter in hand. Fuller and Roberts are both right: in the study start with " the given "; in the pulpit, start with man.

When Dr. Luccock warned against the constant use of " life-situation " sermons, he had in mind " case-presentation " introductions. (See H. E. Luccock, *In the Minister's Workshops,* chs. vi-viii.) All true sermons must be " life-situation " sermons. No part of the Bible properly included in an annual scheme would be other than oriented to the life of God and man. The warning is necessary, however, from the point of view of homiletical *procedure.* The method here suggested is not meant to be a method of presentation. The essential result may be achieved in several ways after the double analysis of Scripture and human predicament has been accomplished. A human situation (a " case ") may be presented and the question raised, Is there anything like this in the Bible? A universal trait of human nature (failing or virtue) may be examined and the way it is dealt with in the Bible introduced. A Biblical story may be so retold as, in the retelling, to become obviously a parallel to human experience. A chapter of church history may be presented in its relevance to the present time as the background for a liturgical occasion, thus relating at once the sermon and the worship. A Greek word, even, brought into relation with common parlance may illuminate the point of contact of the New Testament with our own concerns. The parallel development of a Biblical situation and a modern counterpart may afford another means of demonstrating relevance. Some of these methods (and others) require a particular aptitude on the part of the preacher (e.g., the none-too-common gift of retelling a story), but most of them can be acquired by prayer and the realistic kind of fasting that involves giving up some other activity in favor of attention to this form of preparation. More people are alienated from serious attention to sermons by the failure of the preacher to convey any idea *why* the people should be interested in what he is about to say than by any other cause.

Few can be great preachers, but great preaching is not what is needed. It is *concerned* preaching of which we stand in need, preaching above all by a man who knows and loves his people and is known and loved by them, outside the pulpit as well as in it. I have always found effective and lasting the simple words a young clergyman addressed to us as seminary students. He is now a bishop (the Rt. Rev. Richard Baker) but was then one of a group of alumni selected to return and tell the students what they had learned about the ministry. As befitted a recent graduate, he was modest and brief. He said little more than this: "I have learned that I must love my people while I am writing my sermons." That love is essential, and it means bringing to the task in the study the fruits of every pastoral contact made and every casual observation of people and circumstance on the streets of the town, along with the technical training that remains as an effective possession from college and seminary days.

To love the people in preparing sermons is to bring them into the study at the time. It is of tremendous help actually to visualize certain members of the congregation representative of its different types. For example, in a parish consisting of professors, students, and millworkers, I found it helpful in preparing sermons to consider: Is this intellectually respectable enough to pass the critical judgment of Professor A, Is it interesting enough to expect the attention of student B, Is it understandable enough to reach saintly Mrs. C, who works in the mill by day and tends home and family at night and is too tired to listen unless it seems to her important that she should? That I seldom achieved this ideal is irrelevant. The awareness of the problem is the alphabet of love, and to begin to love is better than a textbook on homiletical devices. For this reason it has always seemed to me worth-while to remind ministers that the opinion of their fellow clergy on their sermons is of much less importance than the opinion of the people and an estimate of the effect upon them of year-by-year preaching. Ministers are, for the most part, poor judges of sermons (even their own) practically by definition, because they so seldom hear sermons from the pews on successive Sundays amid all the tensions of secular life.

It has not always been observed (even by commentators) that the well-known passage called the Hymn of

Love, in I Cor., ch. 13, is primarily and originally concerned with the function and practice of the ministry. In Corinth, there was perhaps no settled ministry of the kind we now enjoy, but chs. 11 to 14 inclusive deal with the conduct of the church in its assemblies. Not merely in the words, "Though I speak with the tongues of men and of angels . . . ," but throughout ch. 13, Paul is saying that any activity of the ministry performed without *agapē* is far worse than useless. This is especially true of preaching sermons because it is true of their preparation. Constant meditation on this passage in context with the chapters that precede it and the one that follows it is more fundamental than any course in homiletics ever devised. While Paul decried the attempt to be men-pleasers, he did not deny the importance of loving them enough to reach them. If ministers would give even a fraction of the serious attention to the preparation of services and sermons and to their presentation that producers give to ordinary radio or television programs, the churches would be revolutionized. When one considers the difference in motives involved and in whose service the effort is made, the contrast needs no further words.

V

THE CLAIM OF THE BIBLE
ON THE PREACHER

BOTH BIBLE and people impose an obligation on the preacher as he stands in the pulpit, and both must receive further attention. The Biblical obligation arises from the service itself. The practice of reading short sections of the Bible in Christian worship is an essential part of the method of Biblical preaching. As a custom it is very ancient. Its use in the Christian church is anticipated by the service of the synagogue. We see this, for example, from the quite detailed and authentic description of the service in the synagogue at Nazareth at which Jesus was invited to read (Luke 4:16-21). It was the practice to make sure that the reading was understood by having, at the most, three verses read in the Biblical Hebrew and then having them "targumed," that is, rehearsed in the vernacular of the congregation. The synagogue custom owed something to the Ma'amad institution, the local gathering of laymen to read the Torah in place of attendance at the Temple. Here the reading to some extent paralleled the Temple rite and in a sense took its place. According to D (II Kings 23:1-3) and P (Neh. 8:1-8), the whole law was read on occasions, but these passages are no guide to the actual practice. They represent to the priestly school the recall of the whole people to the law and of the law in its fullness to the people.

We owe this emphasis on recall and rehearsal of the significant redemptive acts of God originally to the Deuteronomic school. It is clear in the D treatment of prayer and worship in general. Rehearsal of God's past acts in the redemption of his people was a basic element in the approach to God. The liturgical term for this is anamnesis, a memorial rehearsed in order to bring the past with its redemptive action into the present to be lived over again in the experience of the worshipers. In the form of a memorial of Christ's self-offering on the cross, prepared for by a rehearsal of the institution of the Last Supper, it has had a place in the traditional liturgies of Christian worship. An analogy is found in the reading of Ex., ch. 12, at Passover (Easter) in many Christian lectionaries. The whole book of Deuteronomy is, in essence, one anamnesis. Such rehearsal of the pregnant past was (and is) the important feature of the actual celebration of Passover in the home (the Seder). The Haggada associated with the meal was an explanatory commentary applying the events of the past to the present meal and its fellowship. Even when ceremonial acts involving the sacrifice of animals or grain, the pouring of blood, oil, or water, and the eating of flesh were used, the words that were said were interpretive, serving to designate the nature of the act as a memorial of redemptive events and to identify the worshipers with the community of the redemptive covenant.

With the loss of the Temple the Jews came to see that this element of recall and reincorporation could be served by the reading and exposition of the Scriptures apart from the ceremonial. They echoed the words of Hos. 14:2 in offering "the fruit of our lips" (see RSV; in Hebrew and LXX, verse 3). The same attitude, using the same phrase, is found in the Qumrân scrolls, particularly in the Hodayôth, or " Psalms of Thanksgiving." Much of the Old Testament, particularly in the prophetic and didactic books, is adapted to this treatment. It either originated in the form of brief oracles or speeches or has been compiled from previous sources that show the marks of having been used, if not prepared, for oral recitation and remembrance. (For valuable suggestions regarding anamnesis in relation to time, chronological, eschatological, and liturgical, see A. T. Mollegan's Advent chapter in the symposium, *Preaching the Christian Year*. The Jewish background is well handled in C. W. Dugmore's *The Influence of the Synagogue Upon the Divine Office*).

The reading of Scripture and the preaching based upon it is, like the Lord's Supper, a rehearsal and recalling of the redemptive movement of God in human history (*Heilsgeschichte*) in which, for the Christian, the cross of Jesus is central. For this purpose it is not necessary to read a whole Gospel any more than it was necessary for the Jews to read the whole Torah. This is particularly understood when the nature of the Gospels is seen in the light of the modern study of their forms and preliterary development. Sections of the Gospels may be lifted out as we lift out a " clipping " from a newspaper by cutting around its edges. Such a section is aptly called a pericope (which means " cut around "). Not all the gospel material may be so treated with assurance that nothing is lost by the decision as to where the section begins and ends or by detachment from its context. Many passages, however, that may profitably be treated in this way reveal that they once, in all probability, were developed and circulated in the course of Christian preaching and teaching. M. Dibelius' treatment of this aspect of the formation of the tradition in

Chapter 2 of *From Tradition to Gospel* may in itself be read as a study of Christian preaching methods. Many of the sections are in effect " little Gospels," proclaiming the good news in some central aspect. The use of them, therefore, as discreet readings in a service and as a basis for exposition is not an innovation but the recovery of their original purpose.

Concerning the rest of the New Testament the position is not quite so clear. The Epistles, for instance, are more often integrated units of composition. They belong from the beginning to literary development and not to an oral tradition later fixed in writing. Here too, however, the interest of the writers in preaching and teaching has left its mark in a homiletical or paraenetical style, and the material readily falls into manageable units. Paul, in fact, intended his epistles to be read in church (Col. 4:16), and a later writing mentions the effect of the same (II Peter 3:15-16). Lectionaries are very ancient, some so ancient in comparison with extant texts of the New Testament that they help in determining the early state of the text. Justin Martyr testifies to considerable freedom as to the length of readings used and shows that in his time the discretion of the reader was (and presumably could be) relied upon.

The choice of the material naturally varies with the occasion it is meant to serve. This too is an ancient practice, and the reason for its impress on the Scriptures themselves is not hard to find. The transformation of ancient agricultural feasts into occasions of recall and rehearsal produced the Haggadôth, or traditions, necessary for the purpose. Further, many of the significant events and decisive pronouncements took place in connection with the great celebrations of the religious year — for example, Amos' incursions into the festivals at Bethel. The same is

true of the Gospels. Jesus' comments on the life of his people and even his presence in Jerusalem were occasioned
by the festivals of the religious calendar. In the Fourth
Gospel there may well be an element of adaptation of the
material to the calendar and, possibly, in the Synoptics.
The success of Archbishop Carrington's attempt, in *The
Primitive Christian Calendar*, to explain Mark's Gospel on
a lectionary basis is still debatable, but the point becomes
clear that the material as Mark arranged it is, with oc-
casional exceptions, convenient for use in worship or
preaching apart from conclusions based upon the sequence. The most likely origin for this calendrical feature,
where it exists, is the extreme probability that Jesus' activity, like any religious Jew's, was tied into the ecclesiastical (which was also an agricultural) calendar. Western
man in well-watered lands, with efficient storage and
transportation, tends to lose the sense of the desperate importance of these occasions.

Involved in this consideration is the necessity for etiological material, that is to say, passages that describe the
origin of the event celebrated or the practice followed
and that comment upon it in a more or less direct manner.
Hence, for the Christian, there is the reading of the Passion in the week before Easter and the Nativity stories or
the first part of John, ch. 1, at Christmas, the reading of the
institution of the Lord's Supper at the Table celebration
and of the third chapter of John's Gospel or Christ's welcome to the children at a service of Baptism. On other
occasions the possible choice is wider. In the course of
time, the Biblical material used may well come to determine the over-all tenor of the celebration. For instance,
the reading of the story of Jesus' temptations at the beginning of Lent probably owes something to the ancient

practice of using this season as a preparation for baptism (with a warning that the newly baptized must be prepared, like Jesus, for testing — cf. Ecclus. 2:1). In turn, this reading has had a great deal to do with shaping the course of teaching and practice in Lent. Likewise, the reading of the stories of the feeding of the five thousand has probably given to the fourth Sunday in Lent the name "Refreshment Sunday," and the reading of Gal., ch. 4, on the same day the alternative title (in England) of "Mothering Sunday."

Whatever the choice it is desirable, as was said above about the sermon, that the passage be as central as possible to the essential message of the gospel. The Synoptic pericopes have, by and large, this element of disclosing the whole in the part. It seems therefore a sound procedure to start with the selection of material from the Gospels (including the Fourth) and to choose lections from other parts of the Bible because of their value as comment upon it or as background for it. There has been a tendency in modern lectionaries to avoid the typological factor (though currently there is a danger of its overemphasis as a basis for theological exegesis). This is salutary in discouraging a real abuse of the Old Testament, but there are many points at which the typological factor is necessary to the correct understanding of the New Testament literature. The use of such material should be subject to limitation and control. This control is best exercised by confining typological interests to those aspects actually used in the New Testament and to those Old Testament passages which give essential clues to Jewish custom and practice. A good example of the latter would be passages like Ex., chs. 12; 19; 20; Deut., ch. 26; Ps. 118; and Zech., ch. 14, which were associated with the important Jewish occasions. These are a different matter from those which have come to be associated inevitably with Christian holy days through the history of their liturgical use through centuries when typology was the leading form of Biblical theology. The study of this problem can best begin with G. W. H. Lampe's essay in *Essays on Typology.* (Studies in Biblical Theology, No. 22.)

The Epistles and other New Testament works are obviously commentary on the gospel proclaimed in the Gospels and its application to life. These works seem to be more theological in nature. This is often due to the fact that they are addressed to "mixed" groups of Hellenized Jews and converted pagans, less well equipped with a background of Jewish theology than the original audience of Jesus. Many things assumed in the Gospels and necessary in understanding the words of Jesus in an environment other than Palestine had to be spelled out. Both Gospels and Epistles are, however, addressed to the church and not to the world at large. The validity of the attempt to preserve Jesus' teaching in the Gospels is revealed by the fact that there he speaks exclusively (with one or two exceptions, which are obviously just that) to the Jewish church and people. The rest of the New Testament assumes the Christian church as it also assumes the message — the evangel or kerygma — to which it owes its existence and the way of life appropriate to a member of it.

While there is some danger of taking the gospel passages out of context and treating them as secular morality or worldly moral advice, this danger is much aggravated when short passages of the Epistles that deal with the Christian way of life are used. There is no way to avoid this by the choice of passages. To seek to include in one reading Paul's theological basis for his exhortation along with the exhortation would involve reading a major part or even the whole of an epistle. Here the function of the preacher is evident. The church has to lean heavily on his training as an exegete who will treat each isolated passage in its proper context of the entire book and of the New Testament as a whole.

C. H. Dodd's brilliant efforts to recover the heart of the preaching of the gospel in the New Testament, kerygma, and to distinguish it from the discussion of the Christian way of life, didache, has rendered a great service. Yet it would be to misconstrue Dr. Dodd's intention if we supposed that the two could be distinguished in any absolute manner. The proclamation of redemption and the way of life it demands — the kerygma, which serves the one, and the didache, which serves the other — are inseparable in practice. The discussion of the Christian way ("walk" and "conversation" are other New Testament terms) and of the new era and new gifts of life on which it is based form one fundamental assumption. Their separation is a convenient aid to study. The preacher is benefited because he is aware that this separation is a real factor in the minds of his hearers. There the separation is so complete that people are interested in the moral application without any consciousness that it is an *application*. They tend to reject the basic gospel, which gives rise to the application as unnecessary theological embroidery or uncalled-for confusion of "the simple message of Jesus."

Into the origin of the New Testament material a third element enters that here becomes of crucial importance — the apologetic factor. One of the preacher's primary functions is to restore to the consideration of morality its grounding in the gospel and to justify again the connection between kerygma and didache. This is the more

urgently true as modern psychological studies have revealed the real place a sense of guilt (genuine or misplaced) holds in human psychoses and the breakdown of
relationships. We spoke above of the " gap " between ministers and people, and it is nowhere more conspicuous than
in the lay person's almost unconscious refusal to see any
necessary connection between faith and morals, religion
and affairs. Where people do become aware that such a
relation is claimed, they tend to reject it as dangerous interference. Here the apologetic task is pressing. If the
preacher is held close to the Bible, properly exegeted and
applied in relation to his own time, he cannot escape the
obligation to deal with a fissure unknown to Biblical folk.

The choice of passages for worship and preaching, then,
clearly becomes one in which, as was said above, the controlling factor will be the Biblical and kerygmatic message
rather than the attempt to construct liturgically a study
of the human life of Christ. The element of history need
not be lacking. It can be introduced between the Nativity-
incarnation celebration and the observance of the crucifixion-resurrection as these are united by some means of
considering in a methodical manner the works and words
of Jesus. For the most part, the traditional scheme is valid
if it can be delivered from the dead hand of liturgical
archaeology. This bears on those points where an observance is tied fruitlessly to an incidental event or where some
ancient local usage has fastened on the church the use of
Biblical material that raises more problems than the ordinary preacher and congregation should be expected to
deal with. In this category would fall the celebration of
the apostles as individuals who, apart from Peter, are
shadowy figures. Some of them have been traditionally
confused with writers of New Testament books — in which

case it would be more reasonable to celebrate them as authors or Evangelists. It would be better to mark " the Twelve " in one celebration than to indulge in the dubious exegetical and homiletical acrobatics that sometimes occur when the preacher is confronted with the variant lists of " the apostles." In American society the civil and legal calendar is no longer tied to an ecclesiastical one, so that no such confusion would arise as might in England by such revision. It would make more sense for the churches to set aside Sundays for celebrating the establishment of Christian worship at Jamestown in 1607, to emphasize at Thanksgiving the similar theme of 1620 at Plymouth, and to make an effort to redeem from secularism the observance of the Fourth of July, Memorial Day, and George Washington's Birthday.

There are plenty of precedents for the provision of an ordered scheme that can be used by those who are persuaded of its value as a means of guiding preacher and people in the presentation of basic elements in Christian faith and practice based upon the Biblical material out of which these arise. Some such provisions have been criticized for lack of immediate relevance or of immediately apparent connection with the matter in hand. The criticism is often valid, sometimes misguided. We may reiterate that left to himself, the preacher is tempted to turn again and again to " favorite " passages — perhaps determined by the predilections of an honored teacher or by a " school of thought " or by a particular phase of Biblical criticism or theological development. It was objected, for example, that a previous lectionary of the Episcopal Church was composed of the favorite stories of its main architect. Even if this were so, it had two advantages over later lectionaries. First, it provided *narratives* to be read on those Sundays of the year when, in practice, most people attend church and stories are more readily listened to than any other form of discourse. Secondly, the story of salvation in the Bible is presented most significantly in narrative form, the most effective method for the exposition of " the God who acts."

The point to be made applies at this juncture to the need to get the preacher beyond the obvious for the sake of the freshness of his own preaching and the readiness of the people to hear. Not only are the most obvious passages often the least fruitful but those which require a little " digging" often have the salutary effect of " confrontation." That is to say, material that the Biblical tradition and the custom of church usage through the centuries have provided will, as a result of study, often yield results distinctly uncongenial to modern taste. This disturbance of the platitudinous is worth a little further attention.

We may take some extreme examples. In the liturgical churches there has recently been discussion of the so-called Feast of the Circumcision (of Jesus, January 1). Some squeamishness enters into the matter. This kind of delicacy has no place in worship that, if it is to be Christian, ought to be able to deal with facts of physical nature without embarrassment. Without a consideration of circumcision, whether of Jesus himself or of the converts Paul made from paganism, a great deal can be missed. The mention of it is attacked on the ground that it is an outdated problem, irrelevant to Gentiles. This is true. Let us assume, then, that at no time during the church year will the preacher be confronted with the exposition of a key New Testament passage about circumcision. Immediately a whole area of New Testament discussion disappears. A palpable link with history is lost, and the claim of Christianity to be a historical religion is so far weakened.

The fact is that Jesus was a Jew and that he was circumcised. We ought to be confronted with this fact and to deal with it. That he became, as man, subject to the law has a significance that the Pauline Epistles and the Epistles to the Hebrews by no means ignored. Further, the whole question of the inherent nature and immediate future of Christianity in its early days centered around the issue of circumcision. On this point the discussion arose whether the new religion was in fact a new religion, available for all men, or a variant of Judaism confined to Jews. The issue is the universality of Christianity, an issue never more vital than it is today. It cannot be studied in the New Testament apart from the question of circumcision.

Unfruitful, therefore, as a passage on the subject may at first glance appear, a little study reveals its tremendous impact. If the preacher is not asked to deal with it, he may either avoid the subject altogether or else deal with the issues involved in an abstract manner, untouched by the ramifications it had for Paul. A reinvestigation of the matter in the New Testament will raise the significant issues of the true humanity of Jesus, the problems of race and religion, the universal applicability of Christianity, and the relation of faith to religious ordinances and sacraments. Some of these themes, obviously, will come up in other connections, but the fact remains that their New Testament discussion is immediately involved in the context of circumcision. The modern parallels to insistence on circumcision are not far to seek, nor are they, in the long view, less ridiculous for the committed follower of Christ. A study of the subject and homiletical treatment of its results might lead to basing modern demands for brotherhood on something more substantial than assertions that can only doubtfully be supported by the New Testament.

A more central and, in a sense, more urgent example is afforded by the lections for Easter. There has been a widespread tendency to de-emphasize the " empty tomb " arising from attempts to reconstruct the early history of the Christian movement. In this attempt the empty-tomb stories appear as later and tendentious elements. At the other extreme lies the tendency to treat all the stories as pure mythology. From the critical (and certainly from the skeptical) point of view it would be the simplest solution to eliminate all readings that introduce the theme, neither confronting the people with it nor requiring the preacher to deal with it. (I do not know of anyone who has actually suggested the elimination of the *reading* of all the Synoptic and the Johannine accounts, but the ignoring of them in sermons is common.) To do this would immediately ignore the ubiquitous emphasis of the New Testament and substitute for it a modern reconstruction that, to say the least, needs frequent re-examination. A more searching question is to ask why the writers uniformly put the emphasis where they did. To ignore this is to excuse the preacher from the task of justifying the faith at a point where he should explain either why he believes the Gospel accounts to be a fantasy (with whatever purpose) or why he believes such accounts to say something significant about what the faith of primitive Christianity actually was. A purely literal treatment is manifestly impossible.

From an almost opposite direction comes the tendency to concentrate at Christmas on the folk-beloved and commercially exploited story of the Nativity to the exclusion of a discussion of the incarnation. Here the Biblical " myth " can be readily domesticated as the empty tomb cannot. The invasion of the natural order by the Son of

God is repugnant to a scientific age while a subjective faith in immortality is not so uncongenial. The Lukan story, of course, bristles with difficulties, but the issue can be more readily avoided in the general atmosphere of good will and universal fantasy, which even hardened men of commerce indulge in and (perhaps with tongue in cheek) exploit. For this very reason, as suggested earlier, the churches should take the opportunity of presenting in worship and sermon a different approach.

It would be futile to multiply examples. A course of readings carefully avoiding such topics as Jesus walking on the water, the Johannine themes of turning water into wine or the raising of Lazarus, the sharp words of Jesus on the wealthy and on the preference of the Son of Man for the function of a servant, to say nothing of the absolutes about marriage and divorce and about the treatment of "little ones," would be a comfortable lectionary, but it would have the almost disastrous effect of avoiding some of the basic themes of the gospel and remove the stimulus that the preacher sorely needs. The value of the allegorical and mythological elements in the New Testament is not the revival of allegorical interpretation and typological preaching but the fact that they compel the preacher to ask in every generation what the New Testament was trying to say to its generation. It may readily be apparent that what Barth called " the strange new world in the Bible " confronts us. If the key New Testament material is provided and used, there is more often than we care to think an opposition, an " offense," before us, a disparity that at least requires the preacher to stand apart from the current mode and question its assumptions. He is then forced to ask how the gap between Bible and culture may be bridged rather than how he can pretend it does not exist.

The question naturally arises whether this is not likely to be more of a handicap than a help. Should the preacher not be left free to choose points of interest arising from his knowledge of his people and of his times and to select Biblical material (if indeed he uses the Bible at all in preaching) that seems *to him* to throw some light on the matter? An answer can best be given out of experience. What is contemplated is obviously a more distressing task than reading the latest newspaper commentator or the most recent existential or realistic novel. (These have their place but at a different stage of preparation.) The gospel is not determined by the modern state of affairs; nor does even the urgent need of the world for salvation dictate it, but only the understanding of the Bible over against the state of affairs. Preaching involves bringing the two together. In so doing, preaching has a significant part to play in making worship effective. There is no other word for for what a Biblically based preaching, determined by something more than personal preference, can give to the preacher than *independence*. It will compel him always to ask questions, to stand apart from and over against the temporary expedients of the world, release him as far as he can be released from sectional views, and demand from him a heart-searching scrutiny of aspects of the faith uncongenial even to himself. This way lies not popularity but the possibility of being truly an ambassador of another realm.

In the discussion of the relevance of the Bible and Biblical preaching it is necessary to bear in mind the relevance of opposition. If the Bible is not relevant to our situation, it is not true and probably never was. But relevance does not always mean that in every respect the Biblical message fits the world as a glove fits a hand. Relevance may mean bringing to bear what seems, in the current context, new truth, and this comes about only where there is some element of tension. The tension represented by the disparity of the world's way and the Bible's way is not irrelevant — unless it is so to those whose concept of the ministry is that of a " chaplaincy to the *status-quo*."

First of all, the Biblical message is relevant because it deals with the constant. As we saw in the discussion of circumcision, universality may be presented Biblically where it deals with what appears to be a very limited point. This, after all, is a clue to Biblical understanding and essential for any real exegesis. The prophets and Paul were exercised about events immediate to their times upon which impinged the revelation they received and expressed. So, in a different sense, were the Evangelists for whom the great and most pressing event was Christ himself. This is not to say that the Biblical religion, therefore, consists of the derivation of universal principles from a series of trivial considerations, or the abstraction of general truths from temporary experience. Dr. Bultmann made the same point in discussing " viewpoint and method " in his *Jesus and the Word.* " Therefore, when I speak of the teaching or thought of Jesus, I base the discussion on no underlying conception of a universally valid system of thought which through this study can be made enlightening to all. . . . When we encounter the words of Jesus in history, *we* do not judge *them* by a philosophical system with reference to their rational validity; *they* meet *us* with the question of how we are able to interpret our own existence. That we be ourselves deeply disturbed by the problem of our own life is therefore the indispensable condition of our inquiry." (P. 11; Bultmann's italics.)

This understanding means that there is no event or experience of man that is not seen anew in the presence of God's action. There are *constants* (rather than "universals") in the circumstance because it is disclosed that in relation to the incident or behavior involved, God is One and consistent. It is apparent that beneath the local circumstance or the contemporary occasion are concerns with which God is always concerned. There are ways in which men and women behave that God judges or blesses whether they occur in the eighth century B.C., the time of Christ, or the twentieth century A.D. The fact that oppression now can make use of atomic weapons or the revenue from oil wells does not change oppression or God's judgment upon it. The fact that fornication can be safe from detection and from obvious physical results does not change the fact that relationships are distorted and that God is interested in what people do to each other and to themselves. The value of the study of behavior, human and divine, corporate and individual, in an ancient setting, under another culture, in relation to the God revealed in the Bible provides the possibility of a truly objective analysis and understanding. The very differences involved make probable the isolation of the essentials of the matter, enabling us to discern their presence in our immediate time and our outwardly changed circumstances. Changes in the mode of speaking about the enduring facts of life, human and divine, do not alter the facts themselves. Just as an exercise in translation reveals the meaning of idioms, so the task of uncovering the message of God in the Biblical idiom can make us acutely aware of perennial problems.

To these " given " constants the preacher may address himself with confidence that he is dealing with the people before him. It is his duty to make the transition, to hold the Bible up to people and to bring actual people before its mirror, so that they may see themselves naked before God, divested of the protective coloration that modern life seems so ardently anxious to provide. I have always, I hope, profited from the advice offered me by a lay relative when I first entered the ministry. He said, "Address yourself to the universal failings of people and see how you can help them there." Scores of Old Testament and New Testament passages come to mind whose power is basically that they bring under divine scrutiny the familiar behavior of men and women — some of which a curious modern squeamishness (odd in view of Freud and the concentration camps) seems by common consent to avoid or to clothe in romance. With this existential situation the preacher must deal, and should be prompted to deal, by being asked to set the Biblical facts before the people.

The following are two examples: The story in II Sam., ch. 11, of David's accidental falling in love with Bathsheba is romantically told. His schemes to secure her for himself, with or without a husband, and in spite of Uriah's loyalty to his vows as a soldier of David, are dramatically described. Beneath the story there is a keen understanding of human foible and deviousness, naturalness and nobility. It has charm, if a rather grim charm. The Biblical point of view is, at the very end and not until the end, revealed in one simple but devastating word "But." After our absorption with the romance and intrigue, when we have been caught up by the characterization, the whole affair is brought crashing down to reality by the word "But." "But the thing that David had done displeased the Lord." (V. 27b.) *Then* we are ready to read the next chapter, Nathan's parabolic accusation. (The writer of this tale had homiletical skill of a high order.) A somewhat similar New Testament instance is found in Luke 12:16-20 (translated more nearly correctly in the RSV). The fortunate man talks with himself, consulting only himself about his own long-range plans. Suddenly, into this private discourse, comes an unexpected Voice, that of the Listener to all of man's private converse. " But *God* said . . ."

Experience suggests another truth about an ordered use of Biblical material. There is what appears at first to be a deadening repetitiveness about such a plan, referred to above. The same old material comes up again year after year (or whatever the cycle may be). It appears more sensible to seek something new. In their search for the original, preachers have tried to hang their novelties on obscure phrases taken out of context. This is one reason for the disappearance of texts, and a good one. The difficulty, it is my experience, has been exaggerated. About it several things can be said, all of them obvious but also obviously important to remember. The gospel is always new to each generation. The Biblical material (especially today) is almost unknown to each school generation in turn and actually suffers from lack of presentation in its most simple and rudimentary aspects. Those who have heard it before (and in particular those who have accepted it by a lifelong commitment) welcome, like children, a retelling. Again, every passing year, almost every passing day, provides new commentary. A passage that at one point seems remote from current concerns will, with the turn of events, suddenly become a vitally important comment. Anyone who reads the Bible steadily knows this to be true. Some personal examples are: The words of the psalmist, " The overflowings of ungodliness made me afraid " (Ps. 18:4 in *The Book of Common Prayer*, or " Great Bible " version), took on a suddenly new meaning in the midst of the Nazi oppression. So did the words of Pharaoh in Ex. 5:2: " I know not the Lord, neither will I let Israel go."

One need not be superstitious or a fundamentalist to observe that more times than would seem possible, an event in the world, or in the community, or even a circumstance of church life has illuminated as well as been illuminated by a passage appointed for use at that period. There are actually times when this is not at all apparent, when a matter that seems to call for treatment has no obvious relation to the Scriptures at hand. Of course there are emergencies when a particular passage must be substituted, but again, more often than not, study and meditation will reveal a relationship as illuminating as it is unexpected. Those who have taken the way of discarding the provided and seeking the obviously relevant and have not had this experience have, it is fair to say, missed one of the joys of the ministry and lost something of the reassurance that there is " yet more light to break forth from God's word," as John Robinson said to the departing Pilgrims. It is the *latent* power of the Bible that is so astonishing. The relevance so discovered does not belong to the " modern cult of relevance " but to the realm of truth where God's revelation is designed to redeem men in actual history. There is nothing magical about this, and of course common sense must be applied. Too often the power of the Word of God in its impact upon life is missed because we do not believe that the function of the Holy Spirit is to illuminate both the Scriptures and the human scene and that he works effectively when the two are brought together. If the people of the churches are ever to recover for themselves the regular use of the Bible, it will be because the minister has constantly demonstrated that its ordered use can minister effectively to their needs.

A plea has recently been made for exclusively Biblical

preaching in the sense of expository preaching. (See, for example, the effective article by Dr. Paul Van Buren in *The Anglican Theological Review* for October, 1957, " The Word of God in the Church.") The basic reasoning is sound, but serious questions arise as to the wisdom of the method. The exposition of the Bible (or the proper use of a " text") does a great deal to assure the congregation that the preacher is himself " under authority " and that they are not being subjected merely to his own ideas. But simply to expound the Bible is not preaching. Expository discourse requires a particular attention to homiletical principles, and to the relation of the two we must now turn.

VI

THE CLAIM OF THE PEOPLE
ON THE PREACHER

THE NATURE of Christian preaching, thought of as requiring a proclamation by an authorized minister to
a congregation temporarily silent, imposes a serious obligation on the preacher. An equally solemn obligation is imposed by the situation of people caught in the modern culture of the West. In the tension between the two there is
not only the basic problem but a creative opportunity. The
application of what we have judged to be the Biblical
obligation to a situation so widely separated from the Biblical world makes necessary that we should constantly review the homiletical task.

An extreme symptom of the problem is provided by
modern literature. This is a clue to what the intelligentsia
has on its mind. But what is today thought to be *avant-
garde* may also indicate what will be manifest on a more
popular and widespread level in a few years. This literature reveals a reaction against Christianity, but it also involves a reaction against rationality, as such, in which hu-
manism may be as suspect as theism. The McCarthy era
was only symptomatic of a wider development even earlier
manifest beyond the shores of America. The preacher probably cannot, and need not, become really familiar with this
literature, but he would be out of touch with the modern

temper if he were not to some extent acquainted with it. This becomes particularly true at the point where plays and novels of the existential school reach the movie or television screen. If they arrive in a modified or distorted form, it is helpful for the preacher to know that this is so. At this stage, the impact upon the people at large begins to be felt.

The modern American novel is available to a wide public in paperback editions. It deals prominently with people who are at best immoral and at worst degenerate. It will immediately be recognized that to say this is to make a Christian judgment. Such a judgment would not be accepted, probably not even understood, by the " school " represented. The work of this group aims to hold up a mirror to certain aspects of life without making moral judgments, without even a comment. The presentation has an integrity of its own. It would be unrealistic of the pastor to ignore this. It comes within his obligation to try to assess this trend, to estimate how far it represents something more than a cultural fringe, how far it speaks for a basic viewpoint and growing tendency. His Christian attitude cannot be one of mere denunciation. It must be activated by analysis, sympathy, and compassion. Nor should his interest be confined to facile attempts to use the books and plays as " illustrations." He should ask himself whether questions are being asked here that the churches have failed to ask, whether problems are not here posed that it is the serious business of the church itself to raise — and endeavor to answer. In fact, it may well be wise to ask whether novel and play do not present the very questions, *in contemporary form,* that the gospel is designed to answer. Failing this, it is entirely possible that, in spite of the cross at the heart of our faith, we may dismiss the agony so evident in this form of expression and so to a significant extent fail to achieve a deeper and more "related" understanding of our own religion. For this reason, it is to be hoped that there will be a competent development, on a basis of grounding in the fundamentals, of courses in the relationship of the faith to modern literature as part of the curriculum of theological schools — a move in which Dr. Samuel Miller of Harvard has taken an informed part.

For some time past the successful plays on Broadway have shown a concern with what can only be called the "lostness" of modern men and women in their own society. Popular authors like Tennessee Williams make use of the problems of homosexuality, alcoholism, and drug addiction as symbols as well as facts. Sexual promiscuity is almost a commonplace, and Arthur Miller can deal effectively with the suggestion of incestual passion as an element in tragedy (*A View from the Bridge*). In view of a play like *Tea and Sympathy*, one can say that normal sexual relations become almost an act of grace. Monogamous faithfulness and a sacramental understanding of married love are conspicuously absent (not only, of course, in America — see Greene, Camus, Sartre, and Pasternak). Scorn is no answer. An observation closer to the apologetic facts would be that when man rejects the gospel (not to say God), he becomes dehumanized. Yet this serves only to define the problem; it does not deal with it.

In plays and novels, we discover a protest against the dead weight of " the law " in a disintegrating culture, conceived as something imposed by a society that is basically a " closed corporation " and essentially hypocritical. The movement known in England by the term " angry young men," is a protest against the social " establishment." The question whether the Christian church is a bulwark of this society and has outlived its usefulness is a timely one. Plays like *Death of a Salesman, A Hatful of Rain, Cat on a Hot Tin Roof, A Moon for the Misbegotten*, and *The Respectable Prostitute*, and the Camus novels *The Fall* and *The Stranger*, to mention fairly representative examples, make a genuine plea to the Christian (though this is not discernibly their purpose) for compassion. To this category should be added, from another culture, Pasternak's *Doctor Zhivago*. To a significant extent the problem is that of *law and grace*, only it is cast in new terms. Is the law nothing more than the weight of convention, sin not sin except from the standpoint of smug security, and guilt not guilt except by being named so? One cannot help feeling that there is manifest here an ignorance of the gospel (as distinct from "churchiness"), that reveals again the failure to make it heard.

In Beckett's translation of *Waiting for Godot* there is an element of frustration in which humor is so blended with despair that the frustration becomes the manifestation of absurdity. This is brilliantly exhibited in Camus' work (e.g., *The Stranger*) and in Kafka's (e.g., *The Castle*). In the one story, a man guilty of a motiveless murder is condemned to death really because of society's judgment on his attitude toward his mother's death and funeral. In the other, a man, summoned to undertake work for the castle, can neither find out what he is to do nor make his way to anyone who can tell him why he is called. Is this judgment — that the world, as modern man finds it, can most charitably be designated an absurdity — one that the churches can ignore? The cheapening of human life in two world wars, and the sights that those who fought in them saw (conveniently forgotten or suppressed in the national consciousness), is only part of the clue. Modern war no longer stops at the field headquarters; nor does it end when the fighting stops. Everyone is involved, not least a generation of young people raised in homes virtually without parents. The threat of atomic destruction is the death's head at all feasts, and there is an unmentioned bad conscience among those who recall who dropped the first bomb and that people are still dying from its effects. The churches can hardly be said to have given a clear witness in the face of these problems.

To this complex of confusion, it might seem to those outside that preachers have found an answer, but it is suspected that it is an answer found without having really felt the full impact of the question. Therefore, to those with an oppressive sense of the question it seems no answer at all. The type of character portrayed in the literature of frustration and absurdity is uncommonly like the type of people Jesus said would go into the Kingdom of God before the self-assured religious people of his time (Matt. 21:31 ff.). Of what value is the right answer if the basic questions are not being asked? There seem to be so many unexamined assumptions in preaching, assumptions that have long been given a searching analysis elsewhere. This is the essence of the modern apologetic task. A sympathetic understanding of the modern mood may throw a great deal of light on the basic concerns of the gospel and on the problems with which Paul dealt in a quite different idiom. The stage is older than the novel, and from the Greek dramatists to Ibsen and Shaw it has frequently offered searching comments from the side lines of civilization. The chief business of the stage is to entertain, not to provide answers. The chief business of the church is not to entertain but to point the way to the answers.

A solemn aspect of modern literature is the conspicuous absence from its works of any concern with the church and the failure of ministers to appear at all or, if on occasion they do appear, as pathetically helpless, even ludicrous characters without a vital influence on the plot. Nothing could better reveal the judgment that Christianity, as currently understood (at least outside the churches), is *irrelevant* to the real situation. In view of all these factors, we might well ask whether relevance should be dismissed or considered in an entirely fresh sense. There is, after all, a grim absurdity to the Passion of Christ that, existentially presented, could hardly fail to be relevant to the modern predicament. It is even possible that the modern writer might, for all his seeming distance, be nearer the roots of the matter than many modern preachers. (A searching analysis like Sartre's play *No Exit* can hardly be ignored.)

The terrifying aspect of so much modern literature and drama is that nothing happens — that is, nothing happens in the old sense of moral development. Here preaching meets a vacuum when preaching is conceived simply as moral exhortation. The fact remains that Christianity does expect something to happen; it demands a movement rooted in decision and commitment. This gap appears the most difficult of all to bridge. There is, first of all, then, the tremendous need that the pulpit should provide the demonstration that decision — the "leap" of renunciation and attachment — is the essential without which one can only sink more and more deeply into the morass of despair.

This rather special type of literature is only one audible voice in the cry that goes up for the Christian good news of deliverance. Other symptoms have for a long time been apparent. There are, for example, the "lovelorn columns" and other question-and-answer sections of popular newspapers that afford an opportunity for people anonymously to seek counsel. Where the questions are genuine, the counsel needed is that which the churches should preeminently be equipped to provide. Yet if preaching does not encourage people to believe that it will be available in a loving form from a minister not easily shocked or given to denunciation, under the safeguard of secrecy, is it any wonder that people turn elsewhere? The way to the Christian counselor is not so readily opened by advertising or the announcement of "office hours" as it might be by relevant preaching. Anyone who has worked in a community largely populated by students has found this to be true. The loneliness of modern people, even in densely populated areas, is a heart-rending reality. If the churches do not reveal their readiness and capacity to meet this need, other agencies will arise to do so on a less than Christian basis. Preaching has an indirect function here. Counseling cannot be done from the pulpit, but the pulpit can bring the good news that help is available and that it is the kind of help that is needed. We are convinced that the church is the bearer of that good news and the preacher the proclaimer of it. How is it to be made available, how is it to be made intelligible, acceptable, compelling, to modern man? In the last analysis, only by the reproduction in the lives of actual people of the real experience represented by the gospel in its traditional forms.

Here is a fundamental problem. We must be fully aware that the traditional forms are a representation, not the thing itself. The thing itself must always be *represented*. It must use pictures, drama, story, symbol, myth, until it can be acted out and become visible in life after life. (This is, after all, the story of the Biblical revelation — the climax of every effort in an incarnate life.) The representation must speak to the situation in which man finds himself — even if he has put himself into it by his own perversity. That is why it is necessary to speak of "analysis," why David Roberts says we must "start with man," why we are led eventually, though not immediately, to reach the ultimate needs of men (R. H. Fuller) and to deal with their ultimate concern (Tillich). Preaching, even though it can claim to be Biblical, is ineffective as long as it uses forms of representation of the gospel that no longer speak to the people who are being spoken to. In conclusion, therefore, it is necessary to attempt to add to this discussion two things that are impossible — impossible, that is, for anyone to do for someone else. The first is to discuss further the solution of the mythological problem. The second is to give some hints as to methods in preaching.

Each of these is impossible because each preacher, by reason of the very nature of his task, must do it for himself if it is to be authentic (a better word than " sincere "). It is often said that books and courses on preaching are too general. They do not give examples of how it is done. This is true and it is necessarily true. Canon Gordon W. Ireson, in his book *How Shall They Hear?* has attempted to do so, and they are good examples — for him and for his situation. They would be unauthentic if they were more general. They are couched in an English idiom that may sound a little strange to our ears, but this is as it should be. It is the sign of their reality. Canon Ireson may be presumed to know the man with whom he starts and can bring the message to that man. The examples cannot be " lifted," but they do suggest the way of going about the matter. In the same way every preacher must do his own demythologizing, and to that we now turn.

The preacher's business is the expression of a living experience. The problem of the transfer of the experience imbedded in the largely symbolical New Testament terminology and world view has been opened up by Dr. Bultmann's discussion. There is much to be said in criticism and modification of his thesis, and a great deal of it has been said already. (See Bartsch, Henderson, and Jones in the list of books appended.) The problem raised cannot, however, be dismissed. It has to be faced by each generation of preachers and by each individual preacher in a scientific age. Some help might be given in revealing the essential truth behind the New Testament mythology, but in practice this can be done only by exposing the realities of experience. The brand of existentialism employed by Dr. Bultmann may not be accessible or even congenial to us, but the transfer has to be existential — that is, it has to concern immediately present experience. It is not possible to lead people back into the ancient world of thought. A new form of presentation has to be found. The attempt always involves something like a remythologizing in which the preacher is compelled to find modern forms of concretion, modern points of relevance, modern images, modern idioms. Each man must do it to a large extent for himself in relation to the actual people with whom he deals, in their local situation and in the stage of history through which they are passing.

The reason for this is well described by Dr. John Knox in his discussion of the meaning of the cross in *The Death of Christ*. He has discussed two basic ways in which the New Testament writers interpret the death of Jesus in its Christian context. These ways, he holds, are both *illuminating* and *true*. They are both illuminating and true, " not as rational explanations of the fact of Jesus' death, but being

taken much more concretely, as dramatic ways of express-
ing meanings of the whole event of Christ" (p. 151). As
suggested in the first chapter, dramatic ways of presenting
the gospel that at one time or another were "concrete"
in their effect are so no longer. The essential gospel, based
on the Gospels read as God's acts, does not need to be
changed, but it needs to be brought again into focus so
that modern eyes can see that it answers their predicament. As Dr. Knox puts it, the conceptions of atonement
have "a certain logical necessity about them, for they answer to the two ways in which our human need of salvation
is bound to be felt" (p. 151). The *story* of the cross, he
says, "is indispensable and irreplaceable . . . because it
conveys something of the concrete meaning of the deliverance, its quality and its transforming power, and because that quality and that power can be conveyed in no
other way" (p. 154).

Technique is no substitute for the personal discovery of
the fact of deliverance of which Dr. Knox speaks. It comes,
however, to each of us in different ways. We are under
obligation to find out what is at least common if not universal in our own encounter with Christ crucified and risen.
This can be helped by a study of other people's redemptive
encounters. Before these experiences (existential facts)
can be presented to others, they have to be remytholo-
gized. The aim is to recover a concrete and dramatic means
of introducing people to the living Christ so that their need
is met by his power to meet their need. The attempt of the
prodigal son to secure freedom away from home, his
"coming to himself," his return and his acceptance, are all
perennial experiences. The details of the parable — the
third of the estate, the far country, the carob pods and
pigs, the "hired servants," and the like — are not and have

to be transferred to a contemporary idiom. This is not a difficult example because it is in the beginning a human parable. The myth of Christ the Victor through the cross over the demonic powers (one of the ways Dr. Knox mentions) is not so easy; nor is the concept of expiation (the other way) now that slavery and manumission are unknown to us and ritual sacrifices past. These were, to earlier ages, avenues into the power of the gospel; what avenues can be opened for modern man to the same discovery?

There is involved here again what was referred to above as anamnesis. Dr. Knox sees this also. Of the image of Christ the Victor and the image of Christ the Lamb he says, " They are true, because they answer to, recall, actually re-create, real and essential elements in the concrete meaning of the event and the life of the church" (p. 156). Whether a given image still has this power or will have it tomorrow is open to question — a question the preacher must himself try to answer. He can, I believe, answer it only if he engages in discussion with his people, only if he can provide an opportunity for them to say whether this figure or that meets their need. He cannot cling to the images, no matter how hallowed their past, nor how frequently enshrined in stained glass, and insist on their literal truth. What he must discover is how far they have *functional* truth; whether they still operate as they originally did or fail at the very point of application. To quote Dr. Knox once more, " The knowledge does not follow upon the belief that the ancient myths are true; rather we find the myths meaningful and true because the knowledge is given independently of them, although inseparably with them " (p. 156). It is true to say that the vocabulary of Christianity cannot be abandoned. Its rehabilitation, none the less, comes at a later stage in the process and not at the beginning as the initial objective.

This admittedly difficult task of rerepresenting the gospel, in a world so radically different from most of the Christian centuries, cannot be done from the pulpit although that is where it *must* be done. By this I mean that it can no longer be done by the minister alone, an unaided voice. He must, it appears to me, explore in the give-and-take of group dynamics not what the gospel is, but how it may be expressed. Lay people who are " concerned " (who have shared the experience and have begun to adopt the Christian manner of speech) must share the preaching ministry by helping to talk out the images and forms that the pulpit may find possible to use. The peculiar function of the minister is in no way diminished by this consultation with those who are nearer the world than he. He has still the authority of his training, of prayer and meditation, and the duty of safeguarding as well as of declaring the faith. He will still need to be much alone with God and with his books and with *the* Book. He will need behind him the authority of the Bible, as we have argued at length, for fear some aspect of the gospel may be neglected in the enthusiasm for some successful way of presenting this or that aspect of it. But beyond this, in the discovery of points of relevance and of means of communication, the people might well be allowed a larger part.

The function of the people here is not simply that of helping the minister directly. This is bound to have its limitations. Indirect help is enlisted. The possibilities extend beyond those most likely to be of direct assistance (call them " the committed " or " the concerned "). That is to say, groups for the *mutual* study of the Bible, groups for *discussion* of the relation of Christian faith to real areas of life, perhaps informal services not held in the constraining atmosphere of the church, may have a large part to play in enabling people again to hear what is said from the pulpit during worship. To put it another way, perhaps the problem of the modern pulpit cannot be solved *in the pulpit*. Ways and means need to be explored, tried, and discarded, to provide a preliminary experience that will make preaching possible, perhaps the revival of a new form of " catechumenate." At least in these ways the preacher should be able to find out what it is possible for him to do in the pulpit and what it is not possible to do, what forms of expression are failing completely to be understood and which are falling into prepared soil and capable of bearing fruit.

The proper function of the lay people of the churches has not been developed as it should, and every means needs to be explored to enlist them into the authentic ministry of " the priesthood of all believers." (See Dr. Kraemer's *A Theology of the Laity* for a recent attempt to do this.) Some ministers are afraid that by sharing their task their own position will in some way be undermined or devalued. But this is not to be inferred from the extended relationship suggested. There is, necessarily, in the act of preaching a sermon a relationship created — or there should be. Our discussion of authority may have suggested that this is not a relationship all on one level, as if the pulpit and the pew had the *same* function. There will be many aspects of life (for example, as citizens) where preacher and parishioner will be on an equal basis. There will be others in which the hearer (for example, in his capacity as the preacher's physician) will be in a place of authority. In preaching it is not that the preacher has become a dictator nor that he is raised to a higher level of

Christian living (many in the pews may excel him), but that he is, in this relationship for the moment, the interpreter of God's Word.

In the abundant emphasis on "relationship," which has produced the verb " to relate " and oddities like " relatedness," it must be understood that relationship is not an end in itself. R. E. C. Browne brings to our attention that relationship as a sole objective has its dangers. " One of the strengths, and at the same time one of the weaknesses, in this period is concentration on personal relationships which is making them more and more difficult for Christians as well as for non-Christians. At the beginning of this century responsible people were ready to sacrifice the well-being of personal relationships for the furtherance of their lifework; now the tendency is to sacrifice too much for the well-being of relationships. Whenever the maintenance of human relationship becomes an end in itself, it puts such a strain on all concerned that it either breaks or continues at a high spiritual and psychic price paid in large installments by those who devote themselves to the making of the relationship. . . . The ability to maintain relationships depends on a belief about what being human means; from this belief follows the discovery of ways in which those who share a relationship help one another to be human." (*The Ministry of the Word*, p. 96.)

It is a useful view of preaching that it aims to reach people as human beings, to reveal to them their humanity, the humanity redeemed by being taken up into the incarnate life of Christ, to speak to their human situation and lead them to see the glorious possibilities human beings can attain under God. When they have been reached, they can be enlisted to take their proper share in this task through *their* appropriate relationships with one another. The preacher does this, however, not by reducing the gospel to human terms or by stepping aside from his responsibility as a preacher, but by being the means, and the appointed means, of bringing the Word of God first through his *meditation* and then through his *mediation,* to the people as he knows them. His knowledge of them is not simply that secured by "relating" to them as an equal (which of course he will do) but is secured also by the illumination that the Word of God has brought to the human predicament through his ministry. This relationship between minister and people is sacred because it is entirely under the control of the Holy Spirit. It is not a relationship of identical function, not a relationship for relationship's sake, but a relationship that must be created and maintained and enriched because its end is the redemption of men and women from human relationships distorted by sin into that divine-human relationship which is salvation. Its end is life eternal; its fruit is *agapē* or mutual love under the Lordship of Christ.

It was once possible to justify the sermon on the ground that it was the means by which the people could be told in their own speech what was meant by the services at a time when the services were in a language only the priests understood and they not always well. R. C. Petry puts it this way: " To consult the missal is to be reminded that Scriptural materials implanted in the worship of the Christian year constitute a rich thesaurus of things Biblical. Further recognition should be instantaneous that in the awesome services made efficacious in the church's — not the people's — language, the full appropriation of these treasures must be largely dependent on the priestly interpreter, his learning, and his edificatory powers." (*Preaching in the Great Tradition,* p. 99.) What made the function of the preacher (when actually exercised) essential in the Middle Ages now operates in another way. The language of the Bible and of the church is now in the vernacular, but its terminology is increasingly becoming incapable of immediate understanding by modern man. New translations of the Bible and revision of the language used in worship do something to help and, where used, throw an even heavier burden on the pulpit — since the position of the Middle Ages can be practically reversed; the worship may be easier to understand than the preaching! Translation, by itself, cannot bridge the gap between the Biblical way of thinking and modern man's. It goes deeper than language — so that again the preacher has become essential. It is his task to show how things Biblical, theological, and liturgical speak directly to man, and for man to God, by a double method of translation — translation of the " given " into terms of immediate relevance, and translation of modern concerns into terms of needs and problems met by the " given " Christian message.

The need for this sort of discipline suggests that there must be a rather clear idea of the audience to be addressed. This is not so easy as it looks. It might be argued that the speaker at a club or before the Chamber of Commerce, or the teacher before a class of college students, has a much clearer idea of his audience so far as the audience is defined by their reason for being there. A. C. Craig notes: " Preaching to a specialized kind of audience, whatever may be its principle of segregation — whether on the score of age or educational status or particular function and interest — is a different and on the whole an easier matter in which some difficulties are automatically eased, although it has its own special problems. The most exacting occasion is preaching at the regular diet of the church's worship to which the invitation is as wide as humanity itself." (*Preaching in a Scientific Age*, p. 9.) This observation is true in spite of the fact that a real pastor will know the individuals in his audience better; he will have been in their homes and been beside them in intimate emergencies. But this will not cover everyone present.

A casually gathered congregation can contain a wide variety of experience of the faith and of " ability to hear " and, further, of motives for being there. If the preacher is to have a clear idea to whom he is speaking, the motives are important. It need hardly be said that he will preach to those present, not to those he feels should be present or over the heads of the congregation to the community at large. There may be special occasions on which a message to the populace comes within the minister's duty. Even on such occasions it is more effectively delivered *through* the congregation present.

On the other hand, preaching is often inadequate because it is directed to the faithful who would attend in any case. Their faith is established, and they have learned how to worship apart from any failure of the sermon. A sort of incurable politeness attends the efforts of the pastor. " Thank you for your message " — " I enjoyed the sermon " — the ingrained habit of making these remarks prevents any but the most intelligent intimate of the preacher from saying what he actually thinks. Among the regular worshipers are those whose reaction may well be: " Leave us alone. We know all that. Why talk about what we know? " If their attitude is correct, they need to be told *why* they worship and believe so that they may become intelligent witnesses to their contemporaries. From these may be fashioned a growing number of lay " ministers " who will exercise a missionary, apologetical, and pastoral function among their neighbors, fellow workers, and families. Only so can the shortage of ministers in the face of the modern opportunity be really met.

To address the faithful is, one hopes, to speak to only a proportion of those present. Some are there who do not know why they come to church. They happen to be there from habit, from social conformity, or from the feeling that it helps the community if they support the churches. Some are there because they are members of a religious " club," some weekday organization that is the real focus of their attention, and feel they ought to affirm their membership by coming also on Sundays. These may have or might be led to a desire to know why they should come to church, what they should expect from coming, how they may find and give expression to it. They need not only to know but to be given some reason for knowing. There is possibly a minority who come seeking, trying to find again what in childhood or youth seemed to have some meaning, or exploring the phenomenon of " church " for the first time. (There seems to be a new generation of those whom no one has ever compelled to come to church who have discovered that they may come if they wish — and wonder why not?)

The extension of the audience beyond these recognizable groups is a difficult matter. Some of those present may be there as a result of pastoral contacts or the witness of the committed, and there is always this growing edge to be fostered. To address each of the groups mentioned should require a special technique, but to develop one such technique and concentrate on it would largely exclude the others. The weakness of preaching sometimes comes from the sermon's being addressed in any immediate sense to so few of those present. To extend the range of hearing involves the constant effort to find a common ground of concern, alike vital to the faithful, to the habitual, to the clubbers, to the inquirers, and to the chance investigators.

The word " concern " cannot be used without recalling Dr. Tillich's description of religion as " ultimate concern." The judgment first came to me from Studdert-Kennedy that what occupies a person's ultimate and deepest attention is what he really worships. If this is anything short of God, it is, from the Biblical point of view, idolatry. It is open to question whether " ultimate concern " will suffice for a definition of Biblical religion. Its value as a homiletical term can hardly be questioned. Its effect must be to characterize much modern religion as idolatrous. As an apologetic analysis of the current situation, it has the value of starting the discussion from a fresh and realistic point. (An introduction of Dr. Tillich's thought to the public appeared in *The Saturday Evening Post* of June 14, 1958.)

The task of the preacher here is the threefold effort to reveal to men what their ultimate concern at present *is*, the dangers into which it leads if it is a final concern with less than the ultimate, and to lead men to rediscover God as revealed in Christ as the finally worthy and reasonable concern of man — that man was, in fact, created " to glorify God, and to enjoy him forever." The exploration of immediate concerns as symptoms of misplaced ultimate concern presents the preacher with his initial apologetical and evangelical task. This is to put into other words what R. H. Fuller has said about proximate and ultimate needs. The conscious needs of men are symptomatic. Yet it is only through the symptoms that diagnosis, treatment, and prognosis can be attempted.

How can this be done during the sermon? There cannot

easily be discussion by the people there and then. Therefore, there must be in the pulpit some awareness evident
of what might be offered during such a discussion. The
preacher ought to be aware of objections that would be
made, should give them verbal expression, and should try
to deal with them. To say so is virtually to describe a
" diatribe." The term has come to have unfortunate connotations, but it gained this ill repute largely because it
described, not any form of discourse whatsoever, but discourse that was aware of objections. That is to say, the
speaker presented his message with concurrent attention
to the questions and disagreements that those who rejected it would raise. Plato shows Socrates using a dialecti-
cal method of question and answer, but as the answerer is
gradually reduced to monosyllabic agreement, the " dia-
logues " become diatribes in the real sense. We see Paul
using the method in the Epistle to the Romans when he
asks, on behalf of his opponents, " Shall we continue in
sin, that grace may abound? " (Rom. 6:1; see also chs.
3:1, 5, 9, 29, 31; 4:9, 10; 6:15; 7:7; 9:19; 11:1, 11; note how
these differ from the many " rhetorical questions.") It is
a dialogue conducted by one person.

In recent times we have seen attempts to revive this
technique by experiments with " dialogue sermons." In
this form either the preacher takes both parts (an ex-
panded form of the diatribe) or two preachers co-operate.
There have even been experiments in which three people
share the pulpit, the central person representing man and
one on either side taking the part of God and the devil
respectively or the voices of good and evil. (See J. A. Pike
and H. A. Johnson, *Man in the Middle*.) This form comes
close to the revival of religious drama.

Ministers are far too few at the present for these methods to be widely used except on special occasions or by the union of the services of two or more churches. The point, however, is clear. The preacher must show some understanding in his sermons of objections and denials, should anticipate them and try to answer them. He is less likely to make his sermon a " diatribe " in the unfortunate sense of the word if he has discussed the matter with lay people or is treating a subject suggested largely by the difficulties they have expressed. The " clerical " aspect of sermons arises, quite obviously, from the parson's discussion of his own interests and from the defense of the faith against objections that arise from his trained mind rather than from the existential mind of his people. To the expert a preacher who is effective with people may seem at the outset to be dealing with trivialities whereas, to the person in touch with the pastoral situation, these items may be for the people the points of real issue. At all events, they may be effective forms of contact. The opposite error would be to stop there and never get to the message. The test is simply whether the method leads these particular people to the heart of the gospel and not at all whether it corresponds to headings in the theological textbooks.

Some attempt, then, must be made to show this in action. Since it cannot really be done with any hope of not being misunderstood or seeming quite ineffective, let me present it in the nature of an epilogue rather than as part of the text. Before doing so, one other aspect of the distinctly individual nature of the task might be reiterated and a few concluding remarks made.

To return to R. H. Fuller's *What Is Liturgical Preaching?* He has given there examples of the liturgical preaching of selected Gospels and Epistles from *The Book of Common Prayer*. He very properly says of those examples that his exegesis is only the preliminary "spadework" that will not necessarily reappear in the pulpit. This is another warning against taking "untreated" exegesis into the sermon. It is extremely doubtful whether anyone can provide for another a homiletical treatment of any Biblical passage that he can forthwith use. *The Interpreter's Bible* has made a valiant attempt to lead the way to extending exegesis in the direction of exposition. The expositors who are represented would probably be the first to discourage any direct reproduction of their interpretations. It affords an interesting study to note how far the exposition arises out of the exegesis and how far the exegesis permits or encourages exposition. Even if usable exposition could be produced, it should probably not be used verbatim. Every person must bring to the task his own experience. He should bring his present experience, not that of years ago. Even Paul spoke of "his" gospel while he made it abundantly clear there was no such thing. He preached what he had received. He reproduced the kerygma. Yet he makes it clear there was an element of his own experience of Christ that was the mainspring of all his preaching, and it gave him his peculiar sense of authority. No mechanical, liturgical, exegetical, or homiletical device can ever be a substitute for this. Without it a minister is a "professional" in the worst sense of the word and is in danger of being a hypocrite because he is, in fact, as the word meant, acting a part.

This does not mean that a preacher will preach only his own experience. He is there to preach the gospel as his church has received the same. His ordination authorizes him to do so, and a Biblical scheme can implement his authorization. Nonetheless, even his acceptance of what he has not made fully his own is colored, and should be colored, by his immediate experience of God's grace. There can be limited value, therefore, in anyone else's suggestions and none at all in taking them over as they stand.

In conclusion, let me say from the point of view here presented — the importance of an ordered use of the Bible in worship and preaching — that the matter of technique is not less important but more. It is not difficult to find "topics" that will interest people. They do not, however, need to come to church for this. I recall the certainty with which the boys at a large prep school could discern which of the many preachers they were exposed to was doing what he was ordained to do. They were in church and they properly expected to hear about God and in what way he should interest them, not to hear yet another "pep talk," moral discourse, academic lesson, psychiatric analysis, or rhetorical exhibition of "gift of the gab" (as they called it). Their instinct was a true one. The pastor who stands between the needs of his people and the demands of the "given" Biblical passage has a sacred obligation to move back and forth between the two. He can do it only as he develops the ability to analyze the human predicament and to analyze the Biblical material so that the one answers to the other.

The problems posed in the first chapter constitute the special arena in which this must be done and the peculiar aspects of the task at the present time. Modern industry is willing to spend colossal sums on discovering what is on people's minds. To discover this and bring it to expression involves techniques that tend to become fads with a jargon of their own. This should not blind us to the need to experiment with ways in which people can be given preliminary preparation that will enable them to hear the preached gospel. It does not involve falling into the trap of supposing that any such technique can produce the gospel.

The obligation to understand and to make use of modern Biblical studies is in many quarters being minimized or disregarded with the rise of what claims to be a Biblical theology. Yet to retreat into allegorical and typological interpretation means to retreat centuries away from the present time. The response of a generation hungry for authority *at any cost* cannot but leave us sooner or later with a pathetically serious reaction. The real difficulties of the Bible must be faced and out of them won, as I am convinced there can be won, a new basis for an approach to the modern world — a basis that is secure because it has faced the facts and found in the Biblical facts the value of their original purpose. As John Oman once wrote of a man who was tired of the jargon of the pulpit, " The same man who said he was weary to death of hearing of love also said that he had been reading through the Bible with some modern helps and was amazed to find how astonishingly great and interesting a book criticism had made it, as he had never learned from all the ministries he had ever attended " (p. 235).

The third problem, the ethos of the modern world, finds unexpected help in the most "advanced " literature. It would be a curious, and not unlikely, situation if these secular writers more trenchantly exposed the unrealities of modern society than the pulpit ever did. Only as the church recovers its sense of standing " over against " every human structure of society can it escape from being classed (properly) with a culture that has signally failed to give meaning to life. Here the need for the church and its preachers to be confronted always with the Bible is paramount. The loss of audience (actual and more extensively to be expected) is a consequence arising out of the other points. The audience will be recovered when the church provides a preaching so independent and compelling that the news will spread from *within*. It will not be done without experiments aimed at breaking through the traditional system of conducting churches and reaching beyond the ranks of enrolled contributors. In fact, many of the latter will not *hear*, though they are present, until there has come a freshening impact from outside. The best compliment the pastor could hear in many a parish would be for a long entrenched member to say, " I know so few of the people I see in church these days." It might be said with resentment, but the need to say it would indicate that the break-through had begun.

The final word is, as it must always be, that the task is not our task but God's. The people are not our people but Christ's. For them he lived and for them he died. If we truly believe he still lives for them, he will see to it that his gospel does not fail by reason of our failure, but will accomplish that for which he died, whether we ourselves are lost in the process or not. He still speaks. Our only concern is that he might speak *through* us, for the only alternative is that he speak *against* us.

EPILOGUE: GETTING STARTED

B Y FAR the most important question in preparing a sermon will be where to begin. If there is unity and progression, it will be because the introduction has been designed to determine the development and to limit the subject. Very often the question can be answered only by asking first the opposite question, Where is this to end? The beginning is important because sermons so often require the listeners to make a leap. An interest and knowledge is (unconsciously) assumed that is not present. To reach the point at which the preacher starts the modern man has often to divest himself of most of his immediate concerns and reorient his attention. This the preacher neither helps him to do by his introduction nor gives him time to do by his development. It may be put by saying that the preacher is likely to start far ahead of the hearer and to go so fast that the listener not only cannot catch up but can discern only with difficulty where the preacher has gone. The tradition of passive acceptance of the role of preaching lingers on to assure that the preacher has the attention of the congregation when he starts — except for those who through repeated disappointment expect nothing. The problem then is to retain this attention and convert it from politeness into concern and from concern into commitment.

The worship that precedes the sermon should, to some extent, prepare the congregation to " hear " the sermon. The observation only underlines what has already been said about the importance of a preaching arising out of a regular use of the Bible and not limited to the preacher's personal preferences. To make the worship dependent on the sermon, unless the sermon is, in turn, dependent on something more broad than the preacher's interest and choice, would be to reduce the whole service to the level of a deficient pulpit. Apart from this, however, the Bible read in worship still presents a different world, no matter how effectively translated into modern speech. In fact, it is generally true that the more effective the translation the more acute the difference is likely to appear — it is not glossed over by archaic or overfamiliar language. Praise and prayer, also, may have brought the worshiper to penitence and thanksgiving, to a sense of his own needs and those of the world, balanced by joy in the offer of God's salvation. Yet worship too has its own problems of unreality (quite apart from the aggravation of it by sentimental music). What is said, therefore, about preaching can be taken to apply, *mutatis mutandis*, to worship as the framework for preaching. Constant study of ways of relating the two so that they mutually reinforce and elevate each other is clearly an important aspect of the pastoral task.

Let us return to the sermon. Even when the beginning of the sermon has retained the interest of the worshiper, a further problem arises. Can the preacher now confine himself to a theme sufficiently coherent and simple that the listener does not lose track of the subject, become confused, and give up? The more valuable what is said the more likely will an individual hearer pursue the thought for himself. This is an aim achieved. But now comes the test. After some minutes he may return from his reverie to listen again. Can he now discern any connection with what he has been cogitating and what the preacher is now saying?

Just here lies the problem of expository preaching. We can no longer assume passages of the Bible to be well known. Even a text used as a basis for exposition needs to be repeated at intervals if it is to serve as a useful factor toward achieving coherence and unity. Almost any passage of the Bible worthy of exposition in a sermon has a number of facets in itself quite apart from those which occur to the preacher by way of application. It is therefore more than ever necessary that there should be a limitation of the subject, a selection of one line of exposition that will be strictly adhered to, illustrated, applied.

The use of a cyclical scheme has the economical value that other material that comes to mind may be filed for use when the passage in question comes up again. As was suggested above, this leads to deepening insight and a more concentrated, and therefore, simpler development. Here a text can, if properly used, serve as a means of channeling the subject. A good text, however, will also require resistance to the temptation to develop all its possible meanings. It is when a particular theme comes to mind, especially when it comes in the convenient form of one word, that illumination comes and produces unity in the development of the sermon. The result will be ease of delivery for the preacher and ease of listening for the worshiper.

Let us suppose, to use a case within my own experience, that the preacher is concerned because in the local environment, stimulated by press accounts of forthcoming Easter topics, his people have been introduced to ideas about the festival that are certainly not those of the New Testament. Any " liturgical " sermon or any sermon based on his own favorite aspect of the Easter story is likely to run into this difficulty. Anyone hearing what is said may still interpret what he hears in terms of popular ideas that have influenced him. Against this situation the preacher reads over and considers the resurrection narratives and other references in the New Testament. Here, obviously, is no support for belief in the continuance of human personality beyond the death of the body, or for corporate immortality, or for simple living-in-the-memory-of-those-who-are-left, or for the rebirth of all nature in the springtime. Something much more radical is implied and very different from these theories to which the people have been subjected. How express the difference?

Here is the point of bafflement. The preacher cannot (or should not) discuss in the pulpit the nature of the literary phenomena, the state of Jewish beliefs, and the philosophy of matter and spirit. Some more suggestive, more direct, more dramatic theme is necessary to help the worshipers now and provide a clue for future meditation. As the preacher reads and rereads the material, one thing stands out — the New Testament writers all represent the resurrection appearances as *unexpected*. This is one factor always present and can be illustrated from any or all of the stories. But this is not the point at which to start the sermon. The point at which to start is with the people's awareness. It would not be difficult to cull newspaper examples or other instances of the popular denatured views or to describe them in a way the people will recognize as attitudes by which they have at least been beguiled. Then comes the point at which to introduce the Biblical material, limited to the fact that in all the New Testament stories of the resurrection the element of surprise, of the unexpected, is present. Whatever may have happened, however the disciples who recognized the risen Christ did so, whatever may explain the facts, the witnesses were taken by surprise. This element of the unexpected is notably lacking in popular modern accommodations. It can easily be shown how this theory or that could be reached by human invention and for this reason is rather expected than unexpected. Whatever may be said for modern theories, they fail at this point to explain the New Testament message.

The resurrection of Christ and the faith of the church has this element of the unpredictable because it is God at work and he works in his own way and not in ours. Further, however we may conceive our own resurrection hope, it must make allowance for the certainty that we shall be surprised, taken unexpectedly, and possibly unprepared. We can prepare only by becoming acquainted with the presence of Christ in our life now if we are to be ready to meet him in his closer and clearer appearance when God raises us too from the dead. Since this is likely to be a sermon at a Communion service, one can add that God has given us this sacramental means by which to draw near.

Whatever the value of this illustration, the point is that the isolation of one element enables the preacher to deal without distraction with a central aspect of the subject. While it by no means deals with the whole subject, this selection may meet the need of the people to know where the faith of the church differs from popular forms that accommodate it to modern prejudice. By treating a large theme in a limited way the sermon provides a key word to be retained for further meditation.

An obvious homiletical problem arises in the presentation of the Gospels themselves. Whether or not days are set apart for the celebration of saints and Evangelists, the latter deserve to be discussed because of the values to be derived from an understanding of the Gospels as a whole. To do this in full would require a course of sermons. The aim of a single sermon might well be to provide a clue to be pursued in the reading of the Gospels and at the same time provide some application of the gospel itself. There is, for example, the possibility of presenting Mark as a "whodunit" — the gradual disclosure and apprehension of who this is who speaks and acts as Jesus does. The theme of compassion that so clearly animated Luke can be explored or the Johannine emphasis on the glory that comes to climax in the acceptance of the cross.

Recently St. Matthew's Day came on a Sunday. The congregation to be preached to was a strange one to the preacher. What then of Matthew? Clearly a dominant theme in the First Gospel is that of *fulfillment*. The Evangelist treats it in a manner uncongenial to our background, since for him it consists in a rather literal fulfillment of the Old Testament. Yet there is a perennial theme here. "All the people were in expectation" — it is always true. Here then is the place to start, with a discussion of the central place that expectation holds in everybody's life. The hope of fulfillment is fundamental for youth; the loss of it can blight the middle years, and abandoned hope will remove the proper joy of old age. It is surely a God-given trait and one for which God has made provision. Matthew's message is that Christ *is* the fulfillment. Is it not true that without Christ there is no fulfillment? Achievement, success of whatever kind, is often a more real cause of disappointment and a more fundamental problem than is failure. Has not God so ordered life that we will not be satisfied until, like Matthew, we find fulfillment in Christ himself? (The theme can be illustrated from the Gospel quite apart from the Scriptural instances Matthew uses.) The Evangelist was saying of the Jews what Augustine said of all when he affirmed that God has made us for himself and our hearts are restless until they rest in him. This theme has a moden exposition in the personal experience of C. S. Lewis as he describes it in his spiritual autobiography, *Surprised by Joy.*

Let us take a different example. The story of Naaman, in II Kings, ch. 5, presents many difficulties. The story interests the Biblical scholar for its place in the Elijah-Elisha cycle, its indications of the relation of Yahweh to the land, and for the historical developments of the time in which it was set and in which it was written. There may be sermons in these things. On the other hand, the legend itself is symbolical of human pretension and frailties, and it is the preacher's opportunity to show that what may not have happened just so does happen every day. It is a treatment of the human do-it-yourself plan of salvation. An understanding of the small place Israel held among the nations, its subjugation by Damascus and the relative poverty of its land, can help one describe, by contrast, the greatness of Naaman and his pride of place — a successful soldier whose success had brought him wealth and a place of intimacy with his monarch, a man to be envied, yet of whom one thing was true that spoiled all the rest. One word describes it — leper. All his achievement and joy lay under threat. One can hardly avoid thinking of the modern West, with its paradoxes of frustration in the midst of wealth, fear in the midst of power.

There is no need to go through the wonderfully told story here except to suggest how at every point Naaman depended for the solution of his problem on matters that were beyond his own power and, indeed, beneath his notice. They tended to destroy his pride to the point where peevishness almost lost him his chance. He was made to depend on the suggestion of an alien, a slave at that, victim of his successes in the field. He was dependent on the calm but courageous expostulation of his servant. His offered gifts were scorned, his royal letter of introduction was found too overpowering, his splendid presence was ignored by the prophet, and the waters of Jordan ending in the Dead Sea were a poor substitute for the rivers of his own land as they divide to make the country green. It can hardly fail to be a picture of modern man, determined out of his own schemes, ingenuity, triumphs, and self-esteem, to save himself. It would be hard to find a better parable of the humility and readiness-to-accept that are essential to the discovery of redemption. It is not a new sermon theme, but at what period could it have more impact than in the twentieth century? Whether it happened then or not, it happens now — all too often without the same ending.

Sermons are not to be judged by their complete originality. The determination to avoid what has been treated before or said so often leads men to seek out the obscure text and to distort it by separating it from its context. A sermon theme may have been suggested by someone else, but what matters is that it becomes basically our own. I once heard Dr. Reuel Howe, with all his fund of psychological knowledge, preach on Jacob's wrestling in its context. Simply he progressed from Jacob's wrestling with his

brother to his wrestling with himself, to the discovery that
he was wrestling with God. (For all I know this may not
have been original with him; it does not matter, since the
development was assuredly his own.)

The passage presented itself on another occasion when
it was necessary to talk about prayer. It is possible to take
the same progression and use it to show that prayer can
change a man and mark him for life. Jacob might return
home a wealthy, successful man. But before he could do
this, there was a legacy from the past to be dealt with.
He must not only pray about Esau but do something about
him. Jacob's elaborate plans for restitution led him, as
problems of relationship always do, back to himself as his
immediate problem. Yet neither his brother nor he himself was the final issue, since God was concerned with
both. Jacob could not find out the name of his opponent
(and so gain power over him) but did find his own name
changed, always to be a reminder of this occasion. He had,
then, prevailed, but he came back limping. He returned
at peace, but crippled.

Who can expect to meet God and not bear the marks, to
settle affairs before him and not be handicapped? Yet,
chastened, we rejoice because we are at peace with God,
with our neighbor, and with ourselves. The scars were a
part of Christ's resurrection, and they are part of our own.
We shall not cut the fine figure we had imagined, but we
can bear the deprivation when it is the mark of a surrender that is in itself a triumph. So we can understand
how Paul, a New Testament Jacob, could say, " I bear in
my body the marks of the Lord Jesus." We learn before
the cross to accept life on less than our terms and find the
terms better than our own. The story may have been
woven out of a night- or river-demon myth, but its telling

is the revelation of our own encounter with life and God.

The great stories of the Old Testament are sometimes a sounder place from which to start than are those on the higher level of the New Testament. The human figures and situations of the old dispensation are nearer our own people. Old Testament stories need to be introduced, however, in such manner that their relevance to some modern concern is evident enough to justify their consideration. The story of Elijah can, for instance, raise two questions of value for contemporary religious life. The scene on Mt. Carmel (I Kings 18:17 ff.) poses the problem, Is compromise possible? ("How long halt ye between two opinions?" i.e., like a man who sways from side to side.) Generally, compromise is possible and often it is desirable. But there are issues where a choice must be made and adhered to. To fail to choose *then* is to accept the greater evil. The question is always, as the story crudely but forcibly points out, Will God respond? That is the test of insistence. He does respond when we choose God against no-God — not by fire, but by the kindled heart and accepted sacrifice.

Elijah on Horeb (I Kings, ch. 19) provides an example of the life that a wider Biblical context brings to a passage, especially to one that may have become hackneyed by overuse. Why is the "still small voice" important? Horeb here does not stand alone or concern Elijah in isolation. The prophet had run away from the threatening present to the secure past (a species of religious "thumb-sucking"). God asked, "What are you doing *here*, Elijah?" Elijah might have answered that Moses could face Pharaoh but he, Elijah, could not face Jezebel. So he had retreated to Horeb, where God had spoken unmistakably to Moses with signs and wonders. Now again the mountain repro-

duced the ancient signs — wind and fire and upheaval —
but God was no longer giving his word in that way. The
Voice came when all this was over. It sent Elijah back into
the present, where dynasties were to be overthrown, re-
volts and alliances engineered, and his own calling handed
over to another. God, in other words, is not bound by his
own (past) methods. The exigencies of the present are
the place of revelation — or nowhere at all. (We shall
see below that other preachers find the same theme in
the story of Moses.)

It may be observed here that the present task as the
place of revelation may be first applied to the preacher's
own approach to the Biblical material. The Bible becomes
of value to the people when the pastor has found there
the meeting place of present with past, of time with eter-
nity, of man with God. An illustration may be found in the
New Testament. The story of the Wise Men is an example
of the mythological, whether it was so designed by Matthew or not. The value of this legend for preaching lies
not at all in its historicity but in its meaning, a meaning
that becomes useful when the passage is fitted into an ordered scheme. The Magi of Matthew and the shepherds
of Luke can be taken together to represent two different
classes of people, two approaches to the entrance of Christ
into history.

The incidents stand at the opening of their respective
Gospels to make general the result of Christ's advent, and
it is in generalization that their value is found. The stories
may be allowed to speak first to the preacher about his task
and his approach to the differing types of people with
whom he deals. The shepherds were at their work when
revelation came. It is no business of shepherds to listen to
angels in song or to go off in pursuit of a Messianic birth,

but it is not every night that a shepherd's task is enlivened by an invasion from another realm. There are moments when the simplest task is transcended by illumination, and the routine of life can justifiably be discarded to render homage to the fact. For some people revelation breaks into their ordinary days with a song, and, surely, to lift people's hearts above the commonplace in an age of dreary routine work must be a prime concern of the pastor in worship and preaching. He, too, is to "go to Bethlehem" and return to tell the people what he has seen so that wonder may be restored to ordinary life (Luke 2:17-18).

The Magi, on the other hand, became aware of the star (so the story) in the main line of their proper occupation, astrology. Astrologers were the ancient counterpart of the modern scientist. What broke into the shepherds' routine as revelation came to the Magi in the pursuit of their profession as a discovery. Before preaching a sermon on revelation and discovery, the preacher should consider that this reflection speaks to him. It teaches him that his task is to lead some people to find God through their vocation and others in spite of their occupation.

Herod also comes into this legend. The new fact of the Christ unites shepherds, Magi, and king. Herod, too, had an interest in the Child. The contrast of this interest with that of the Wise Men may be purely legendary, but it is an observable fact. The world of power is one thing; the world of humble pursuit of the truth is another. The threat to entrenched position produces the response of violence now as in Herod's time; the personally costly following of truth to see where it leads produces the religious spirit of homage and offering — and here, we fear, preachers have much to learn from pure scientists.

In neither of these cases was the story written for these purposes. Its probable purpose was to say that Christ comes to "the quiet in the land" (Luke's favorite birth-narrative emphasis) and his coming is discovered by the stranger while it is misconceived and rejected by the official in his palace (Matthew's point — see also Luke's parable of the Samaritan). The process of remythologizing what is already legendary is a more authentic undertaking than to allegorize the parabolic (see my *The Jesus of the Parables*) or to "typologize" the historical. It is hard to escape the thought that Matthew was intentionally offering contrasts. Meditation on them reveals how deep they go and suggests sermon topics that serve the Evangelist's purpose and can be illustrated elsewhere in his Gospel — which is an obvious criterion that we have read him aright.

The story does not actually say that the "three kings" followed the star across the desert. They had been motivated by the star's appearing but had followed their own usual train of reasoning, running in the rut of custom. For this reason, they assumed that the place to find a prince would be at the royal court. It was from Herod's court to "where the young child was" that they were led by the star — from the place to which their usual way of thinking had led them to the place where the star, the motion of another world, came to rest. "When they saw the star, they rejoiced with exceeding great joy." Is it far-fetched to see that what this suggests is that it is so often our own interpretation of what begins as revelation that leads us to the wrong place? If we are not aware of the difference, we end up in Herod's palace instead of at the place of Christ's manifestation.

That this and other stories of the Bible must speak first

to the preacher about his task was suggested earlier con-
cerning I Cor., ch. 13. It is the preacher's duty to consider
this direct relationship before he " sermonizes " a passage.
Reference has been made to the modern tendency to treat
Palm Sunday merely as a celebration of Jesus' entry into
Jerusalem. In the traditional lectionaries the triumphal
entry is the gospel for Holy Communion on the first
Sunday in Advent, the opening of the ecclesiastical year.
In other words, Jesus first appears as the Lord who comes
to his Temple — and cleanses it. Two related passages
come to mind. " The Lord whom you seek will suddenly
come to his temple. . . . But who can endure the day
of his coming, and who can stand when he appears? . . .
he will purify the sons of Levi." (Mal. 3:1-3.) On this,
apart from the story of the cleansing of the Temple itself,
there is a New Testament comment. " For the time has
come for judgment to begin with the household of God."
(I Peter 4:17.) There could hardly be a better theme with
which to start the Christian year. It is the church that must
first suffer when Christ draws near, judged for the neglect
or fulfillment of its vocation. The parables and many of
the sayings of Jesus, when they are read as addressed to
Israel as church, have the same impact. Likewise, the
preacher must first subject himself to the message of the
Bible before he hastens to apply it to his people. It can
define for him his task and induce in him the humility
that will make him a leader of the people in their proper
ministry rather than an authoritarian critic of their ways.
It is this kind of " sincerity," rather than that of the performer, which he seeks — to sit himself humbly before the
Word that it may speak to him and through him rather
than that he should presume to speak for it. It would be
good for us to meditate this Advent theme before begin-

ning each annual round of sermons.

This is possible because the Bible is a preaching book. For example, it is not possible to take the sequence of sections as they appear in the Gospels to be the sort of chronological arrangement produced by an eyewitness or by historical recollection. It is important to remember that they are preaching units. It may be worth-while to recall that one pericope follows another because the "complex" so arranged had preaching value for the early church. Fairly obvious examples would be the two "dinner-table" sequences in Luke 7:36-50 and ch. 14:1-24. In these Jesus deals with the exclusiveness of the self-assured and related topics. They do not make good dinner-table conversations, but they make sense as complexes developed in preaching on a theme.

The same may be said of passages in the Gospels that are obviously composite from the point of view of literary and historical criticism but are found in this form because they were welded in preaching. The story of the paralytic already mentioned (Mark 2:1-12) will serve as illustration. It deals fundamentally with Christ's power to set a man free. The paralytic cannot do anything for himself, cannot demonstrate any qualifications for forgiveness. Being carried in by the faith of others and walking out carrying his own bed are the two extremes. Between comes no exhortation to do something for himself, but first the releasing words, "Son, thy sins be forgiven thee." Jesus does not deal with the symptoms but with the cause of the paralysis. It is no use to say, for example, to the alcoholic, "Your trouble is you drink too much; give up drinking." This is exactly what he cannot do. It is necessary to restore confidence, to remove the reason for his flight from reality. When that is done, the residual habit can be dealt with. It is a gospel of grace we preach, not of moralistic exhortation. If the story was originally two, a healing narrative and an apology for the claim to forgive sins, the combination represents most probably the experience of the church that the forgiveness proclaimed in Christ's name set men free to do what their sense of guilt had prevented their doing. It is apologetic based on testimony, expressed in dramatic form. As such, it is available still for the preacher's purpose wherever the church has the like experience of the releasing power of faith in our Lord.

The power of the gospel stories to diagnose the human situation can be illustrated by the story of Zacchaeus in Luke 19:1-9. Consideration will show that to be short is not an obstacle. If one is well liked, the crowd will give place to let the small of stature through. But a tax collector for an alien government (whether Herodian or Roman) did not find his way of life likely to win him friends or invite consideration. Zacchaeus' problem was not his stature but his choice of profession and his practice of it. The climax of the story is Jesus' judgment: "He also is a son of Abraham." Zacchaeus, the rejected, has been accepted, brought within the holy fellowship, even though to do so had caused Jesus to risk the scorn of the population. (So, in Jesus' parable, the prodigal son was received back as son, not hired man). By sharing Zacchaeus' exclusion, Jesus had made it possible for Zacchaeus to become a sort of one-man community chest for the city.

When such a story is reduced to its essentials, we see its relevance. The problem of rejection and acceptance, which, in the churches as well as in the world, is based on even less significant things than a man's profession, weighs down and breaks many people. The gospel tells us we are accepted as we are, not as a result of a status

achieved by our own endeavors. The cost of our acceptance Christ has borne. From the other angle, to reject
others in order to maintain our own precarious standing
of self-esteem is to make it unlikely, if not impossible,
that they can be redeemed to serve the common good.
"While we were yet sinners, Christ died for us" — that is
true, but it needs to be made important and understandable by becoming the answer to an experienced human
situation. We find it necessary to talk of the results of sin
and the symptoms of guilt before we can apply the rem-
edy. Sin and guilt are abstractions until we can demonstrate from their immediately discernible circumstances
that they exist. A more than superficial reading of the Gospels will show that this is also the level at which the Gospels preach the gospel: not in theological abstractions, but
in existential encounter.

The most effective preachers have behind their pulpit
discourse the ability to see the relevance and, by analysis
on two levels, to bring the Biblical message and human
experience together. It is of value to read the sermons of
masters of the art, past and present, not to assimilate their
"points," still less to borrow their illustrations, but in order to study their methods — one for his introductions,
another for his style, this one for his use of analogy, the
other for his skill with development of a theme. In some
cases a man will find a kindred spirit who can be a perma-
nent inspiration and model. The best preacher I have
known told me that his own style had been learned by
study of a particular preacher, and I should judge that for
his time and place he had outstripped his master. It is
helpful to find that other people have dealt with the same
theme, the same passages of Scripture, sometimes in sur-
prisingly the same way. Biblically based sermons would be

a difficult matter for strict copyright.

Doubtless others have found the series of incidents in Mark, ch. 5, an illuminating presentation of progressive attitudes toward Jesus. "What have I to do with thee? . . . torment me not." (V. 7.) "They began to pray him to depart out of their coasts." (V. 17.) "He that had been possessed with the devil prayed him that he might be with him." (V. 18.) "He fell at his feet, and besought him greatly, . . . I pray thee, come. . . ." (Vs. 22-23.) "If I may touch but his clothes, I shall be whole." (V. 28.) It is not impossible that the incidents are thus arranged with a purpose. I discover that David Roberts has noted much the same thing in Luke, ch. 8. He uses what I have called the method of double analysis. In his case, the analysis of the three incidents he chooses is paralleled with three revelations of the human situation. What emerges is Christ as Tormenter, as Healer, and as Liberator. His sermon is called, " Three Pictures of Christ."

We can find in Dr. Roberts another example of the method in the sermon " Christian Freedom." His theme is Rom. 8:1-2, an analysis and comparison of Christian freedom with freedom cut away from its Christian roots. The sermon arises, however, from an examination of the New Testament dilemma of the responsible man who is at the same time man enslaved. It is from this that he comes to his text and not the reverse.

Dr. Paul Scherer is a very different type of preacher, but his method is fundamentally the same. He has a gift for combining the double analysis in a quite remarkable and kindling way. It is clear in his sermons that the analysis has always first been thoroughly done. Insight into the Biblical material has been met by penetration of the human situation. It is the meeting of the two about which he invariably speaks. He can start with the Bible, as many people cannot or should not, and start there successfully because he immediately puts the listener into it and the listener is at once interested. Frequently, his sense of modern man's predicament enables him to show the difficulty and *difference* of the Biblical text and the opposition becomes illuminating.

He is one of the preachers who dealt with Moses — in the sermon that gives the title to a collection, *The Place Where Thou Standest*. His theme is the modern conspiracy against the present. His ability to sketch in a few vivid sentences the story of Moses, his character and situation, leads to the core (for his present purpose) of the story — "where thou standest is holy ground." Here, where we are now, is where the task begins. It is not surprising that a truly Biblical theme can make use of many incidents in the Bible. I remember, for instance, hearing much the same point made by the late Dean Phillips on the text "What is that in thine hand?" Other starting places will occur to others who discover that the Bible insists that "now is the day of salvation" and that the existential is the place of destiny.

Dr. Scherer as a Lutheran knows the discipline of an ordered year. The Collect for the Twentieth Sunday After Trinity contains the words, "keep us, we beseech thee, from all things that may hurt us; that we, being ready . . ." He has read in this connection (the Epistles for this part of the year are based on it) the Epistle to the Ephesians. He has noted that the author there urges the abandonment of many things that people take refuge in. But he does not start there. He begins his sermon: "There is a sense, it seems to me, in which we may say quite truly that the fundamental urge of human life is the urge to get through this world, so manifestly a dangerous place, as safely as may be. That's why we want homes and work and health. It's why many people want God really. We are looking for some kind of security in the desperate face of life, some cushion against the too great hardships of our being here." Then he is ready to introduce the Scripture as he has seen it. So he proceeds, " Now if you will carefully examine what Paul is trying to tell the Ephesians, there in the fourth chapter of his letter to them, you will find that he's urging them flatly to get rid of the things in which they have taken refuge." (P. 39.)

The sense Dr. Scherer so often manifested (for instance, when I used to hear him in the early thirties) was how the Bible quite frequently cuts right across our pet assumptions. This has been referred to above as, in itself, a form of " relevance." It is interesting to read what a layman writes about the task of preaching in mid-century. He is a newspaper columnist, Sydney J. Harris, writing under the date line Chicago, Illinois, in the *Des Moines Register,* for July 27, 1957. He says, " It seems to me that no pastoral task is harder than composing a weekly sermon that is lively without being trivial, and solid without being dull and didactic." He goes on to say that the trouble with sermons is not always that preachers are " ponderous " but that religion is thought of as feeling and not fact. " But religion is a way of thinking as well as of feeling. It is an idea as much as it is an emotion. And it is a provocative, radical, a revolutionary idea, if you trouble to examine it down to the roots. The purpose of preaching, I have always thought, is to make people feel uncomfortable, to challenge their easy assumptions about life, to provoke not a vague feeling of good will toward God but to become a more reasonable and loving creature of God.

To do this effectively, the preacher needs a lively sense of history, a firm grasp of psychology, and enough humor to make the congregation swallow the bitter pill of self-scrutiny." He adds, " It is difficult for me to imagine a more formidable weekly assignment."

Mr. Harris is surely correct. The task is made harder when the preacher supposes that if only the gospel is clearly presented (with perhaps charm and humor as well as clarity), people will accept it. It is not the assumption of the Bible that everyone who is sick wants to be well, that everyone who is " beat " wants to be saved, that everyone who is lost wants to be found and brought home. The Fourth Gospel puts on the lips of Jesus the question to the impotent man in John 5:6, " Do you wish to be well? " (so the Greek). The demoniac in Mark, ch. 5, referred to above, who wanted Jesus to leave him alone — presumably because he preferred his present state — has many modern counterparts. Can they be saved in spite of themselves? Is part of their salvation the giving to them the desire to be saved? The same demoniac was soon begging to be allowed to follow Jesus. On the other hand, the paralytic in Mark 2:1-12 could not indicate what his choice would be until his real problem had been dealt with. The Bible has a strange power to illuminate the Bible, and this can be discovered by constant reading with meditation and by holding it up to life as a mirror. The men and women we see there *are* reflections, and it is with their contemporary opposites that we start.

The better known and more popularly verbalized a text is the more difficult it is to make it come alive. Matthew 6:24 is as widely known as it is ignored. " No man can serve two masters. . . . Ye cannot serve God and mammon." We can see that the theme is a single aim through complete trust. We consider that few of our people reject God, nor do they surrender entire to the world. Yet Jesus seems to have envisaged an even more dangerous condition that better describes the majority of Christians — "God and . . ." Here again is a place to start. There are plenty of illustrations around us of "hyphenated Christianity" — "God and my country," "God and my family," "God and my race," "God and myself." Christ is not put aside entirely and the world embraced, but a variously mixed proportion of each is attempted. Perhaps for us this is inevitable as a start. But this is what Jesus dealt with when he said that to serve (not to admire, but to serve) God *and* mammon is impossible. Out of this predicament, then, people must be won to move on. "Purity of heart," said Kierkegaard, "is to will one thing." People can be brought to a readiness to hear what our Lord says if we can lead them from where they are with a sense on their part that we understand and that (they will think, "therefore,") the Bible understands.

The Bible does help us to understand when it suddenly illuminates the situation. Its distance from the modern involvement often helps. Imaginative dwelling on the material in a framework of prayer will often do it. The great issues come to us casually for the most part. What, for instance, did Pilate think as he put on his robes that Friday? "Another day on the bench. More rioters to deal with. Every day the same . . ." ? It was simply in the course of the day's work that he found himself confronted with the inexplicable — and became enshrined in the creeds as a date line, "under Pontius Pilate." The thought suggests the importance of a prepared day, offered to God at the start, so that whatever arises we may meet it with him — pre-eminently so for the preacher who can never be apart from his task.

To be prepared, that is, expectant that God will use the Bible to reveal, will awaken reflections of the issues of life, is a sound clue to the task of the pulpit. Most of the rules may be summed up in reality by the observation that what we see we can tell others about. That is why a discussion of preaching can never be concluded. The task is yours and it is mine and each one's individually. The meeting place with God is next Sunday's material. It may reveal something we have already seen, but we shall see it newly reflected, newly illuminated by the people we serve. It is for them. God designed it so. We receive it so. They await it. Salvation has many facets. Men and women, we ourselves, are to be saved, if at all, where we are and in relation to the issues of our present lives and persons and acquaintanceship. That is where the task lies. And, "Lo, I am with you always, to the close of the age" is the assurance of our high calling when we put ourselves under orders to his Word.

BOOK LIST
AND REFERENCES

The following books, in the order of their use, are referred to in the text and those noted are the sources of quotations.

CHAPTER I

Wedel, Theodore O., *The Christianity of Main Street*. The Macmillan Company, 1950.

—— *The Pulpit Rediscovers Theology*. The Seabury Press, Inc., 1956. Quoted by permission of the publishers.

Brooks, Phillips, *Lectures on Preaching*. E. P. Dutton & Co., 1877. (Reissued as *Eight Lectures on Preaching*, edited by J. R. T. Moorman, S. P. C. K., London, 1959.)

Whyte, William H., Jr., *The Organization Man*. Simon and Schuster, Inc., 1956. (Paperback edition, Doubleday Anchor Books, 1957.)

Packard, Vance O., *The Hidden Persuaders*. David McKay Company, Inc., 1957.

Riesman, David, Glazer, Nathan, and Denney, Reuel, *The Lonely Crowd*. Yale University Press, 1950. (Paperback edition, abridged, Doubleday Anchor Books, 1953.) Quoted by permission of Yale University Press. Page references are to the Yale University Press edition.

CHAPTER II

Justin Martyr, *First Apology*, chapter 67. Edited and translated by Edward R. Hardy in The Library of Christian Classics, Vol. I. The Westminster Press, 1953.

Dodd, Charles H., *The Apostolic Preaching and Its Development*. Harper & Brothers, 1949.

Farmer, Herbert H., *The Servant of the Word*. James Nisbet & Co., Ltd., London, 1941; Charles Scribner's Sons, 1942. Quoted by permission of the publishers.

Brunner, Emil, *The Scandal of Christianity*. The Westminster Press, 1951.

McArthur, A. Allan, *The Christian Year and Lectionary Reform*. (Cited as, "The Christian Year.") S.C.M. Press, Ltd., London, 1958. Quoted by permission of the publishers.

Browne, R. E. C., *The Ministry of the Word*. (Studies in Ministry and Worship.) S.C.M. Press, Ltd., London, 1958. Quoted by permission of the publishers. (Available in the U.S.A., Alec R. Allenson.)

Cope, G., Davies, J. G., and Tytler, D. A., *An Experimental Liturgy*. (Ecumenical Studies in Worship, No. 3.) John Knox Press, 1958.

Knox, John, *The Integrity of Preaching*. Abingdon Press, 1957. Quoted by permission of the publishers.

Dillistone, Frederick W., *Christianity and Symbolism*. The Westminster Press, 1955.

Barth, Karl, *The Word of God and the Word of Man*, translated by D. Horton. The Pilgrim Press, 1928.

Chapter III

McArthur, A. Allan, *The Evolution of the Christian Year*. The Seabury Press, Inc., 1953.

Johnson, Howard A. (ed.), *Preaching the Christian Year*. Charles Scribner's Sons, 1957.

Fuller, Reginald H., *What Is Liturgical Preaching?* (Studies in Ministry and Worship.) S.C.M. Press, Ltd., London, 1957. Quoted by permission of the publishers. (Available in the U.S.A., Alec R. Allenson.)

Ecumenical Studies in Worship. John Knox Press.

No. 1. Cullmann, Oscar, and Leenhardt, F. J., *Essays on the Lord's Supper*. 1958

No. 2. Garrett, T. S., *Worship in the Church of South India.* 1958

No. 3. Cope, Davies, and Tytler, *An Experimental Liturgy.* 1958

No. 4. Nicholls, William, *Jacob's Ladder: The Meaning of Worship.* 1958

No. 5. Herbert, A. S., *Worship in Ancient Israel.* 1959

Milik, J. T., *Ten Years of Discovery in the Wilderness of Judaea,* translated by J. Strugnell. (Studies in Biblical Theology, No. 26.) Alec R. Allenson, 1959.

Eliot, T. S., *Murder in the Cathedral.* Harcourt, Brace and Company, Inc., 1935. Quoted by permission of the publishers.

CHAPTER IV

Coggan, F. D., *The Ministry of the Word.* Canterbury Press, London, 1946.

Lewis, C. S., *A Preface to Paradise Lost.* Oxford University Press, London, 1949.

Scott, R. B. Y., "Is Preaching Prophecy?" *Canadian Journal of Theology,* Vol. I, No. 1.

Howe, Reuel L., *Man's Need and God's Action.* The Seabury Press, Inc., 1953.

Smith, Charles W. F., *The Jesus of the Parables.* The Westminster Press, 1948.

Lewis, C. S., *The Screwtape Letters.* The Macmillan Company, 1946.

Roberts, David, *The Grandeur and Misery of Man.* Oxford University Press, Inc., 1955. Quoted by permission of the publishers.

Luccock, Halford E., *In the Minister's Workshop.* Abingdon Press, 1944.

CHAPTER V

Dugmore, C. W., *The Influence of the Synagogue Upon the Divine Office.* Oxford University Press, London, 1945.

Dibelius, Martin, *From Tradition to Gospel,* translated by B. L. Woolf. Charles Scribner's Sons, 1934.

Carrington, Philip, *The Primitive Christian Calendar.* Cambridge University Press, Cambridge, 1952.

Lampe, G. W. H., and Woollcombe, K. J., *Essays on Typology.* (Studies in Biblical Theology, No. 22.) Alec R. Allenson, 1957.

Bultmann, Rudolf, *Jesus and the Word,* translated by Louise P. Smith and Erminie Huntress Lantero. Student's edition. Charles Scribner's Sons, 1958. Quoted by permission of the publishers.

Van Buren, Paul, " The Word of God in the Church." *The Anglican Theological Review,* Vol. XXXIX. No. 4. October, 1957.

CHAPTER VI

Gassner, John (ed.), *Best American Plays,* Fourth Series (1951–1957). Crown Publishers, 1958. Contains Anderson, Robert, *Tea and Sympathy;* Gazzo, M. V., *A Hatful of Rain;* Miller, Arthur, *A View from the Bridge;* O'Neill, Eugene, *A Moon for the Misbegotten;* Williams, Tennessee, *Cat on a Hot Tin Roof.*

—— *Best American Plays,* Third Series (1945–1951). Contains Miller, Arthur, *Death of a Salesman.*

Camus, Albert, *The Fall.* Alfred A. Knopf, Inc., 1958.

—— *The Stranger.* Alfred A. Knopf, Inc., 1946.

Pasternak, Boris, *Doctor Zhivago.* Pantheon Books, Inc., 1958.

Beckett, Samuel, *Waiting for Godot.* Grove Press, 1954.

Kafka, Franz, *The Castle.* Alfred A. Knopf, Inc., 1947.

Sartre, Jean-Paul, *No Exit* and *Three Other Plays.* Vintage Book, 1958. Includes *No Exit* and *The Respectable Prostitute.*

Ireson, Gordon W., *How Shall They Hear?* S. P. C. K., London, 1958.

Knox, John, *The Death of Christ.* Abingdon Press, 1958. Quoted by permission of the publishers.

Kraemer, Hendrik, *A Theology of the Laity.* The Westminster Press, 1958.

Petry, Ray C., *Preaching in the Great Tradition*. The Westminster Press, 1950.

Craig, A. C., *Preaching in a Scientific Age*. Charles Scribner's Sons, 1954: S.C.M. Press, Ltd., London. Quoted by permission of the publishers.

Tillich, Paul, "The Lost Dimension in Religion." *The Saturday Evening Post*, June 14, 1958.

Pike, James A., and Johnson, Howard A., *Man in the Middle*. The Seabury Press, Inc., 1956.

Oman, John W., *Concerning the Ministry*. S.C.M. Press, Ltd., London, 1936. Harper & Brothers, 1937. Quoted by permission of the publishers.

EPILOGUE

Lewis, C. S., *Surprised by Joy*. Harcourt, Brace and Company, Inc., 1956.

Scherer, Paul, *The Place Where Thou Standest*. Harper & Brothers, 1942. Quoted by permission of the publishers.

Harris, Sydney J., Column, "Strictly Personal," *Des Moines Register*, Des Moines, Iowa, July 27, 1957. Copyrighted by General Features Corporation, New York, New York. Quoted by permission.

FURTHER SUGGESTED READING

Communication

Dillistone, Frederick W., *Christianity and Communication*. William Collins Sons & Co., Ltd., London, 1956.

Kraemer, Hendrik, *The Communication of the Christian Faith*. The Westminster Press, 1956.

Dillistone, Frederick W., "Evangelical Symbolism."

Jamieson, Graham, "Communicating and Relating in Religion."

Dunkel, W. D., "Theology in the Theater."

All in *Theology Today.* Vol. XVI, No. 1. April, 1959.
Evangelization of Modern Man in Mass Society. Pamphlet
of the World Council of Churches, October, 1949.

The Current Scene

Benoit, J.-D., *Liturgical Renewal.* (Studies in Ministry and
   Worship.) S.C.M. Press, Ltd., London, 1958.

Butz, Otto (ed.), *The Unsilent Generation.* Rinehart & Company, Inc., 1958.

Davies, H., *A Mirror of the Ministry in Modern Novels.* Oxford University Press, Inc., 1959.

Howe, Reuel, *The Creative Years.* The Seabury Press, Inc.,
   1959.

MacLeish, Archibald, *J.B.* Houghton Mifflin Company, 1959.

Mueller, William R., *The Prophetic Voice in Modern Fic-
   tion.* Association Press, 1959.

Packard, Vance, *The Status Seekers.* David McKay Company, Inc., 1959.

Tillich, Paul, *The Shaking of the Foundations.* Charles Scribner's Sons, 1948.

Demythologizing

Bartsch, H. W. (ed.), *Kerygma and Myth,* translated by
   R. H. Fuller, S. P. C. K., London, 1953.

Blackman, E. C., *Biblical Interpretation.* The Westminster
   Press, 1959.

Henderson, Ian, *Myth in the New Testament.* (Studies in
   Biblical Theology, No. 7.) Henry Regnery, 1952. Alec R.
   Allenson.

Jones, G. V., *Christology and Myth in the New Testament.*
   George Allen and Unwin, Ltd., London, 1956.

Mascall, E. L., *Words and Images.* The Ronald Press Company, 1957.

Throckmorton, B. H., Jr., *The New Testament and Mythology.* The Westminster Press, 1959.

New Testament Words

Barclay, William, *A New Testament Wordbook*. S.C.M. Press, Ltd., London, 1955.

—— *More New Testament Words*. S.C.M. Press, Ltd., London, 1958.

Enslin, M. S., "Preaching from the New Testament: An Open Letter to Preachers" in Johnson, E. S. (ed.), *The Joy of Study*. The Macmillan Company, 1951.

Fox, Adam, *Meet the Greek New Testament*. S.C.M. Press, Ltd., London, 1952.

Richardson, Alan, *A Theological Word Book of the Bible*. The Macmillan Company, 1951.

Preaching and Worship

Coggan, F. D., *Stewards of Grace*. Hodder and Stoughton, London, 1958.

Easton, B. S., and Robbins, H. C., *The Eternal Word in the Modern World*. Charles Scribner's Sons, 1937.

Forsyth, P. T., *Positive Preaching and the Modern Mind*. Independent Press, London, 1949.

Pelikan, J. J., "Luther on the Liturgy," and Prenter, R., "Luther on Word and Sacrament," in *More About Luther*. Luther College Press, 1958.